FAISAL MALIK

Trials and Tribulations

An Islamic Perspective

Ta-Ha Publishers Ltd

مَا وَدَّعَكَ رَبُّكَ وَمَا قَلَىٰ

"Your Lord has not abandoned you
Nor does He hate you" 93:3

© Faisal Malik 1442 AH/ 2021 CE
First Published in September 2022

by:
Ta-Ha Publishers Ltd,
Unit 4, The Windsor Centre,
Windsor Grove, West Norwood,
London, SE27 9NT
United Kingdom
Website: www.tahapublishers.com

All rights reserved.
No part of this publication may be reproduced, stored in any retrieval system, or transmitted in any form or by any means, electronic, mechanical, photocopying, recording or otherwise, without the prior written permission of the publishers.

Written by: Faisal Malik
General Editor: Dr. Abia Afsar-Siddiqui
Book and cover design: Shakir Abdulcadir ✦ opensquares.uk

A catalogue record of this book is available from the British Library
ISBN: 978 1 915357 04 5

Printed and bound by: Mega Basim, Turkey

CONTENTS

Introduction	7
The Nature of Trials and Tribulations	10
We were created to be tested	13
Our whole life is a test	15
This whole world is a place of test	16
Being tested in ease and hardship	17
Know the Nature of this Life	26
Preferring this life over the afterlife	27
Dipping one's finger in the sea	29
Like a traveller	31
A prison	32
A worthless thing	33
A cursed delusion	34
Chasing a shadow	36
Names and Qualities of Allah ﷻ	40
The All-Knowing	42
The Most Generous	46
The Omnipotent	50
The Most Merciful, The Most Compassionate	53
The Most Loving	55

Benefits of Trials and Tribulations — 58
   Your sins will be removed — 60
   Your heart will be guided and purified by Allah ﷻ — 61
   The trial will make you stronger — 63
   Allah ﷻ loves you — 65
   Allah ﷻ is raising your status — 66
   Receive the blessings, mercy and guidance of Allah ﷻ — 67

The Path of the Blessed — 70
   Prophet Ayyub's ﷺ sickness — 75
   Maryam's *(alayhas salaam)* pain — 76
   Prophet Yaqub's ﷺ separation — 77
   The best of creation — 79

How to Deal with Trials and Tribulations — 82
   Du'a — 83
   Prophetic Supplications — 90
      Du'a of Umm Salamah ﷺ — 90
      Du'a of Prophet Yunus ﷺ — 91
      Entrusting your affairs to Allah ﷻ — 92
      Seeking refuge from anxiety and grief — 93
      Seeking refuge from sorrow and distress — 94
      Spring of the heart — 94
   Qur'an — 96
   Dhikr — 99
   Istighfar — 104
   Salawat — 107
   Taqwa and Tawakkul — 109
   Sabr — 111
   Shukr — 112
   Serve the deen of Allah ﷻ — 113
   Keep company with the righteous — 116
   Remember your final abode — 117

Recommended Reading — 118

INTRODUCTION

We begin in the name of Allah ﷻ, to Whom all praises belong. The Most Compassionate, The Most Merciful, The Source of all good, The One Who relieves our worries, Who heals all wounds, Master of all that exists, Who knows us more than we know ourselves and to Whom is our ultimate return.

Why am I suffering?
Why does God allow evil to exist?
Why do bad things happen to good people?

These are questions that have plagued human existence since the beginning of time, across all cultures and civilisations. Various philosophies and religious traditions have tried to provide answers to the question of human suffering by reflecting on its origins, why it exists and how best to deal with it.

Having a meaningful understanding of evil and suffering can allow a person to develop proper coping mechanisms, not only to tolerate the challenges of life, but to use trials and tribulations as an opportunity for spiritual, psychological and intellectual growth. In turn, the reverse is also the case where an inability to understand the metaphysical realities that underly human suffering can lead to a crisis of faith and loss of peace of mind. There is evidence to suggest that there is a strong connection between Muslims that fall into a crisis of faith and their inability to develop an Islamic understanding of the tragedies that they may experience in life:

> *…we find that the inability to process tragedy within a religious framework may be the root cause of doubt.*[1]

By the grace of Allah ﷻ, this book will seek to bring to centre stage those teachings found in the Qur'an and Sunnah that will allow us to gain a better insight into who we are, why we were created, the nature of trials and tribulations and how to deal with difficulties in this life, through the following six sections:

- The Nature of Trials and Tribulations
- The Nature of this World
- Names and Qualities of Allah ﷻ
- Benefits of Trials and Tribulations
- The Path of the Blessed
- How to Deal with Trials and Tribulations

These teachings have been a source of strength for millions of Muslims throughout the centuries in the face of hardship. Through the simplicity of this book, it is hoped by the will of Allah ﷻ, that the reader will begin to have a direct relationship with the Qur'an and Sunnah, which in turn will provide strength and guidance for the reader throughout their life.

---

1 Youssef Chouhoud, *Modern Pathways to Doubt* (Yaqeen Institute, 2016) p.20 https://yaqeeninstitute.org/youssef-chouhoud/modern-pathways-to-doubt-in-islam/

We ask Allah ﷻ to allow us to reconnect to His book and the teachings of the beloved Messenger ﷺ and allow them to be a means of catching us when we fall, strengthening us when we are weak and guiding us when we are lost. Ameen.

We ask Allah ﷻ to accept this work, forgive our shortcomings and provide us with sincerity to work only for His sake. All praise is for Allah ﷻ. Any good that has come from this humble work is solely from Him and any mistakes are mine and from the accursed shaytan.

The Nature of Trials and Tribulations

What is the true nature of trials and tribulations and what role do they play in our lives? Despite the fact that trials and tribulations are an inevitable part of human existence, we misunderstand their role and nature within our lives. This misunderstanding leads us to be ill-equipped to handle the challenges of life in a manner that is healthy. The assumption for many is that our lives are meant to be care-free and devoid of difficulty, and any hardship we endure is an aberration from what otherwise is meant to be a problem-free existence.

We tend to perceive our lives in this way despite the fact that we witness people going through hardships around us on a daily basis. One just needs to just turn on the news, visit a hospital, go to a busy part of town and see homelessness, visit a graveyard or simply listen to the struggles of people around us to understand that tests and trials are not a stain on an otherwise untroubled existence; rather they are an embedded and integral part of human life on earth. This reality is highlighted in several places in the Qur'an and hadith, that make it clear that tests and trials are not only a certainty but also a central part of our existence.

وَلَنَبْلُوَنَّكُم بِشَىْءٍ مِّنَ ٱلْخَوْفِ وَٱلْجُوعِ وَنَقْصٍ مِّنَ ٱلْأَمْوَٰلِ وَٱلْأَنفُسِ وَٱلثَّمَرَٰتِ وَبَشِّرِ ٱلصَّٰبِرِينَ

We will test you with a certain amount of fear and hunger and loss of wealth and life and fruits. But give good news to the steadfast.

(Surah al-Baqarah 2:155)

In this ayah of the Qur'an, Allah ﷻ has stated He ﷻ will certainly test us. Furthermore the verbal form of the Arabic verb 'to test' has an additional ل and ن which serve to bring out emphasis. In other words, Allah ﷻ has emphasised that He ﷻ will certainly test us and those tests can take the form of fear, hunger, loss of wealth, lives and fruits. Ibn Kathir, the renowned commentator and scholar of Islam, explained that to be tested in 'lives' can refer to the death of loved ones, while some early scholars believe that it can refer to sickness and disease. He also explained that 'fruits' can refer to gardens and fields that do not produce crops as expected, while other scholars mention that it can refer to children.[2] Whether the term 'fruits' refers to children or to agricultural produce, it alludes to the notion of the failure to see the expected results of hard work and effort. It is a reality in this world that we will often work towards a goal and not see the anticipated outcomes materialise.

We were created to be tested

إِنَّا خَلَقْنَا ٱلْإِنسَٰنَ مِن نُّطْفَةٍ أَمْشَاجٍ نَّبْتَلِيهِ فَجَعَلْنَٰهُ سَمِيعًۢا بَصِيرًا

We created man from a mingled drop to test him and we made him hearing and seeing.
(Surah al-Insan 76:2)

---

2   Ibn Kathir Dimashqi, *Tafsir Ibn Kathir* (Dar Al-Kotob Al-Ilmiyah, Beirut, 2012) Vol.1, p.181

From the very beginning of our existence, when we were no more than just a microscopic entity invisible to the naked eye, it was determined that we would be tested by our Lord, our Creator, Allah ﷻ. In addition, Allah ﷻ informs us that He ﷻ created our very state of life and death as a test to see which of us is best in deeds:

He who created death and life to test which of you is best in action. He is the Almighty, the Ever-Forgiving.

(Surah al-Mulk 67:2)

Our whole life is a test

We created man in trouble.
(Surah al-Balad 90:4)

In addition to being created to be tested, humans are, by default, created in a state of trouble. Among some of the early Muslim scholars, this ayah was interpreted as meaning human beings are in a state of hardship, difficulty and long suffering.[3] While some may experience more difficulty than others, this highlights the fact that all human beings are created to be in a constant state of struggle, even if that struggle may not seem apparent to others. For instance, even the wealthiest person has to work hard to maintain his wealth, status, security and, perhaps most importantly, his peace of mind.

So while humans do not have the option of bypassing difficulties, we do however, have the choice of how we wish to direct those efforts; in other words, which goals warrant going through struggles for. We can choose to toil for the temporal things of this life, which will very soon vanish, or we can choose to toil for that which is everlasting – the eternal abode of the next life, al-akhirah.

---

3 Ibn Kathir Dimashqi, *Tafsir Ibn Kathir* (Dar Al-Kotob Al-Ilmiyah, Beirut, 2012) Vol.4, p.444

This whole world is a place of test

إِنَّا جَعَلْنَا مَا عَلَى ٱلْأَرْضِ زِينَةً لَّهَا لِنَبْلُوَهُمْ أَيُّهُمْ أَحْسَنُ عَمَلًا وَإِنَّا لَجَٰعِلُونَ مَا عَلَيْهَا صَعِيدًا جُرُزًا

We made everything on the earth adornment for it so that We could test them to see whose actions are the best. We will certainly make everything on it a barren wasteland.

(Surah al-Kahf 18:7-8)

Often when we experience difficult periods in our life, we dream of escaping to a place of ease and security. We idealise that another city or country would be the ideal place to escape our difficulties and achieve all our dreams as the saying goes, "The grass is greener on the other side." While indeed some places may provide more solace and comfort for our lives than others, the reality is that this whole world is a place of test and Allah ﷻ has adorned what is on earth in order that He ﷻ may test us. We should never be deluded into thinking any place on this planet is perfect or worry-free; the only place where perfection exists is in paradise. Regarding this world, Ibn Ata'illah said:

> *Do not be surprised when difficulties happen in this worldly abode. This is the nature of life.*[4]

Being tested in ease and hardship

Another major misconception in the minds of many is that it is only when we experience hardships and difficulties that we are being tested. However, from the Qur'anic perspective, moments of ease and comfort also constitute great tests for us:

---

4   J. Auda, *A Journey to God, Reflections on Hikam ibn Ata'illah* (Awakening Publications, UK, 2017) p.34

فَأَمَّا ٱلْإِنسَٰنُ إِذَا مَا ٱبْتَلَىٰهُ رَبُّهُۥ فَأَكْرَمَهُۥ وَنَعَّمَهُۥ فَيَقُولُ رَبِّىٓ أَكْرَمَنِ وَأَمَّآ إِذَا مَا ٱبْتَلَىٰهُ فَقَدَرَ عَلَيْهِ رِزْقَهُۥ فَيَقُولُ رَبِّىٓ أَهَٰنَنِ

As for man, when his Lord tests him by honouring him and favouring him, he says, "My Lord has honoured me!" But then when He tests him by restricting his provisions, he says, "My Lord has humiliated me!"

(Surah al-Fajr 89:15-16)

These two ayat in Surah Fajr describe both states – when one is given blessings and when one's provisions are restricted – as a state of ابْتَلَىٰ (test), indicating that both prosperity and adversity are tests from Allah ﷻ.

The ayat preceding this passage (6-14) speak of the nations and people that had wealth and power, such as 'Ad and Thamud, and their corruption. The ayat following this passage (17-20) go on to condemn those do not honour orphans, do not feed the poor, devour inheritance and have an insatiable love of wealth. These are the crimes that are associated with having too much wealth and being ungrateful for one's blessings. For those that understand, this is a realisation that material comfort and abundance are in some ways a greater form of test. It is easier to become heedless and greedy at a time of plenty and it is at this time that people often fail in the test by being ungrateful and becoming arrogant.

The idea of wealth and material comfort being a trial is further supported by the hadith:

وَاللَّهِ لَا الْفَقْرَ أَخْشَى عَلَيْكُمْ وَلَـٰكِنْ أَخْشَى عَلَيْكُمْ أَنْ تُبْسَطَ عَلَيْكُمُ الدُّنْيَا كَمَا بُسِطَتْ عَلَى مَنْ كَانَ قَبْلَكُمْ فَتَنَافَسُوهَا كَمَا تَنَافَسُوهَا وَتُهْلِكَكُمْ كَمَا أَهْلَكَتْهُمْ

'Amr ibn 'Awf ﷺ reported that the Messenger of Allah ﷺ said:
By Allah, it is not poverty I fear for you, rather I fear you will be given the wealth of the world, just as it was given to those before you. You will compete for it just as they competed for it and it will ruin you just as it ruined them.
(Sahih Bukhari and Muslim)

The Prophet's ﷺ Companions (sahabah) understood the warning of this hadith very well and that may be why we find many instances of them highlighting the dangers of this material world. 'Abdur Rahman ibn 'Awf ؓ said:

$$\text{ابْتُلِينَا مَعَ رَسُولِ اللَّهِ ﷺ بِالضَّرَّاءِ فَصَبَرْنَا ثُمَّ ابْتُلِينَا بِالسَّرَّاءِ بَعْدَهُ فَلَمْ نَصْبِرْ}$$

We were tested with hardship alongside the Messenger of Allah, peace and blessings be upon him, and we were patient. Then we were tested with prosperity after that and we were not patient.
(Sunan at-Tirmidhi)

This statement of 'Abdur Rahman ibn 'Awf ؓ, himself a wealthy companion of the Prophet ﷺ is very profound. It highlights that when the sahabah were in a state of persecution and poverty in the early stages of Islam, they were able to remain steadfast and even they found patience difficult to practice at times of prosperity.

Yet again, we are reminded in the Qur'an:

يَـٰٓأَيُّهَا ٱلَّذِينَ ءَامَنُوا۟ لَا تُلْهِكُمْ أَمْوَٰلُكُمْ وَلَآ أَوْلَـٰدُكُمْ عَن ذِكْرِ ٱللَّهِ ۚ وَمَن يَفْعَلْ ذَٰلِكَ فَأُو۟لَـٰٓئِكَ هُمُ ٱلْخَـٰسِرُونَ

You who believe! Do not let your wealth or
children divert you from the remembrance of Allah.
Whoever does that is lost.
(Surah al-Munafiqun 63:9)

إِنَّمَآ أَمْوَٰلُكُمْ وَأَوْلَـٰدُكُمْ فِتْنَةٌ ۚ وَٱللَّهُ عِندَهُۥٓ أَجْرٌ عَظِيمٌ

Your wealth and children are a trial
but with Allah is an immense reward.
(Surah at-Taghabun 64:15)

Even though children and wealth are allowed in Islam and are among the great blessings of the world, if a person loves his children and wealth more than Allah ﷻ then these things will be a source of spiritual failing for an individual. The Qur'an even commands Muslims not to compare their own wealth and children with that of the disbelievers, who seem to be enjoying a life of luxury. In reality, their material well-being is just a cover for their psychological turmoil, which they experience by neglecting their soul and its relationship with Allah ﷻ.

فَلَا تُعْجِبْكَ أَمْوَٰلُهُمْ وَلَآ أَوْلَٰدُهُمْ إِنَّمَا يُرِيدُ ٱللَّهُ لِيُعَذِّبَهُم بِهَا فِى ٱلْحَيَوٰةِ ٱلدُّنْيَا وَتَزْهَقَ أَنفُسُهُمْ وَهُمْ كَٰفِرُونَ

Do not let their wealth or children impress you. Allah merely wants to punish them by them during their life in this world and for them to expire while they are unbelievers.

(Surah at-Tawba 9:55)

It is quite interesting to note in this regard that many secular lands, where religion has minimal influence, are lands of great wealth and material comfort. At the same time, however, these are also the same countries in which the prevalence of inner discontent is high.⁵ This indicates that material well-being, when not connected with God-consciousness (taqwa), will be a source of trial and torment.

In another ayah of the Qur'an, Allah ﷻ states that He ﷻ will test us with both evil and good as a fitna, highlighting the reality that tests come both in times of ease and difficulty.

Every self will taste death. We test you with both good and evil as a trial. And you will be returned to us.

(Surah al-Anbiya' 21:35)

---

5 Gallup Polls from 2005 and 2006 show that countries that are more religious tend to have lower suicide rates. https://news.gallup.com/poll/108625/more-religious-countries-lower-suicide-rates.aspx

This ayah further gives solace to the believer by mentioning that we will return to Allah ﷻ; no matter how difficult the tests of life get, death will put an end to the suffering for the righteous.

An important concept that is mentioned here is **fitna**. To fully understand this term and its import on human suffering, it would be helpful to look into its linguistic usage. Fitna – فِتْنَة – has the trilateral root ف ت ن and the verb fatana – فَتَنَ – has the meaning of 'to burn' in the context of smelting gold and silver.[6] This is the process of purifying these metals by putting them in intense heat to burn away the impurities and leave behind only the pure substance.

From this, we can better understand that the purpose of trials and tribulations is to purify our souls. It is through the intensity of trials that we turn to Allah ﷻ and become more conscientious about performing righteous deeds and it is through this process that we can become spiritually purer and better versions of our selves.

The verbal form of the word fitna occurs in Surah Ta-Ha, when Allah ﷻ speaks of the test that He ﷻ has given some people in the form of abundance.

---

6   E. W. Lane, *An Arabic-English Lexicon* (Librairie du Liban, Beirut, 1968) Vol. 6, p.2334 and Imam Al-Raghib Al-Isfahani, *Mufradat Alfaz ul-Quran* (Dar Al-Qalam, Damascus, 2009) p.623

وَلَا تَمُدَّنَّ عَيْنَيْكَ إِلَىٰ مَا مَتَّعْنَا بِهِۦ أَزْوَٰجًا مِّنْهُمْ زَهْرَةَ ٱلْحَيَوٰةِ ٱلدُّنْيَا لِنَفْتِنَهُمْ فِيهِ وَرِزْقُ رَبِّكَ خَيْرٌ وَأَبْقَىٰ

Do not direct your eyes longingly to what We have given certain of them to enjoy, the flower of the life of this world, so that We may test them by it. Your Lord's provision is better and longer lasting.

(Surah Ta-Ha 20:131)

Interestingly the command to control one's gaze occurs in the Qur'an in two scenarios: one is the command for believing men and women to lower the gaze in the context of modesty with the opposite gender and we are told that this is *purer* (Surah an-Nur 24:30-31). In the above ayah, we are instructed to control our sight by not looking longingly towards those that have been granted more material wealth than us. Again, this is a means for our purification, as it prevents the love of materialism from entering or taking root in our hearts.

Know the Nature of this Life

Preferring this life over the afterlife

Prophet Adam ﷺ originally dwelt in paradise, a place of eternity and perfection; and as the children of Adam ﷺ, we have an innate longing for paradise, which was our original home. This life is a place of struggle and hard work, through which, by the Mercy of Allah ﷻ, we can return to paradise. However we, as humans, are often impatient and instead of seeing this life as a bridge to return to our original home, we seek perfection and permanence in this world. But that effort is futile and will only cause pain since this world is neither perfect nor permanent; everything in this life has its flaws and will one day come to an end. The Qur'an, in many places, warns people against preferring the life of this world over the next:

بَلْ تُؤْثِرُونَ ٱلْحَيَوٰةَ ٱلدُّنْيَا وَٱلْءَاخِرَةُ خَيْرٌ وَأَبْقَىٰٓ

Yet you still prefer the worldly life, when the Next World is better and longer lasting.

(Surah al-Ala 87:16-17)

Allah ﷻ warns against loving the things of this world more than loving Him ﷻ, the Messenger ﷺ and striving in His ﷻ path:

قُلْ إِن كَانَ ءَابَآؤُكُمْ وَأَبْنَآؤُكُمْ وَإِخْوَٰنُكُمْ وَأَزْوَٰجُكُمْ وَعَشِيرَتُكُمْ وَأَمْوَٰلٌ ٱقْتَرَفْتُمُوهَا وَتِجَٰرَةٌ تَخْشَوْنَ كَسَادَهَا وَمَسَٰكِنُ تَرْضَوْنَهَآ أَحَبَّ إِلَيْكُم مِّنَ ٱللَّهِ وَرَسُولِهِۦ وَجِهَادٍ فِى سَبِيلِهِۦ فَتَرَبَّصُوا۟ حَتَّىٰ يَأْتِىَ ٱللَّهُ بِأَمْرِهِۦ ۗ وَٱللَّهُ لَا يَهْدِى ٱلْقَوْمَ ٱلْفَٰسِقِينَ

Say, "If your fathers or your sons or your brothers or your wives or your tribe, or any wealth which you have acquired, or any business you fear may slump, or any house which pleases you, are dearer to you than Allah and His Messenger and striving in His way, then wait until Allah brings about His command. Allah does not guide people who are deviators."
(Surah at-Tawba 9:24)

In truth, human beings only give preference to this world over the next because they fail to see the reality of the next life against the reality of this world. If we truly understand the nature of this world, we would never give it the importance that we do, and we would no longer hopelessly put our efforts into it at the expense of the hereafter.

Dipping one's finger in the sea

مَا مَثَلُ الدُّنْيَا فِي الْآخِرَةِ إِلَّا مَثَلُ مَا يَجْعَلُ أَحَدُكُمْ إِصْبَعَهُ فِي الْيَمِّ فَلْيَنْظُرْ بِمَ يَرْجِعُ

Al-Mustawrid ﷺ reported that the Messenger of Allah ﷺ said:
What is the example of this worldly life in comparison to the Hereafter other than one of you dipping his finger in the sea? Let him see what he brings forth.
(Sahih Muslim)

Imagine the insignificance of this world that it is not even equivalent to a drop of water in relation to the vastness of the next life! Whatever we experience in this life is nothing compared to the afterlife as the following hadith shows:

يُؤْتَى بِأَنْعَمِ أَهْلِ الدُّنْيَا مِنْ أَهْلِ النَّارِ يَوْمَ الْقِيَامَةِ فَيُصْبَغُ فِي النَّارِ صَبْغَةً ثُمَّ يُقَالُ يَا ابْنَ آدَمَ هَلْ رَأَيْتَ خَيْرًا قَطُّ هَلْ مَرَّ بِكَ نَعِيمٌ قَطُّ فَيَقُولُ لاَ وَاللهِ يَا رَبِّ وَيُؤْتَى بِأَشَدِّ النَّاسِ بُؤْسًا فِي الدُّنْيَا مِنْ أَهْلِ الْجَنَّةِ فَيُصْبَغُ صَبْغَةً فِي الْجَنَّةِ فَيُقَالُ لَهُ يَا ابْنَ آدَمَ هَلْ رَأَيْتَ بُؤْسًا قَطُّ هَلْ مَرَّ بِكَ شِدَّةٌ قَطُّ فَيَقُولُ لاَ وَاللهِ يَا رَبِّ مَا مَرَّ بِي بُؤْسٌ قَطُّ وَلاَ رَأَيْتُ شِدَّةً قَطُّ

Anas ibn Malik ﷺ reported that the Messenger of Allah ﷺ said: That one amongst the denizens of Hell who had led a life of ease and plenty amongst the people of the world would be made to dip in Fire only once on the Day of Resurrection and then it would be said to him: "O son of Adam, did you find any comfort, did you happen to get any material blessing?" He would say: "By Allah, no, my Lord." And then that person from amongst the persons of the world be brought who had led the most miserable life (in the world) from amongst the inmates of Paradise and he would be made to dip once in Paradise and it would be said to him, "O son of Adam, did you face any hardship? Or had any distress fallen to your lot?" And he would say: "By Allah, no, O my Lord, never did I face any hardship or experience any distress."

(Sahih Muslim)

The above hadith shows us the true insignificance of this life in relation to the next. If a person lives to a hundred years and their entire existence on earth was filled with hardship, the memory of that suffering will evaporate in the face of the infinite bliss awaiting them in the next life. Whatever number is divided by infinity becomes nothing since the finite is just an illusion in relation to the infinite. After we die, all that we experience in this life will seem as if it were an illusion, a dream. There is a saying attributed to 'Ali 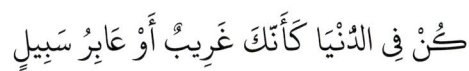: *People are asleep and when they die they wake up.*[7]

Like a traveller

Ibn 'Umar 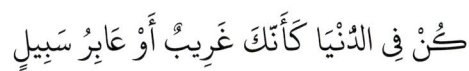 reported that the Messenger of Allah 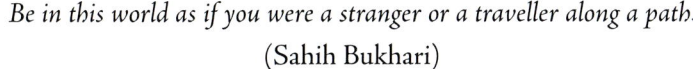 said:

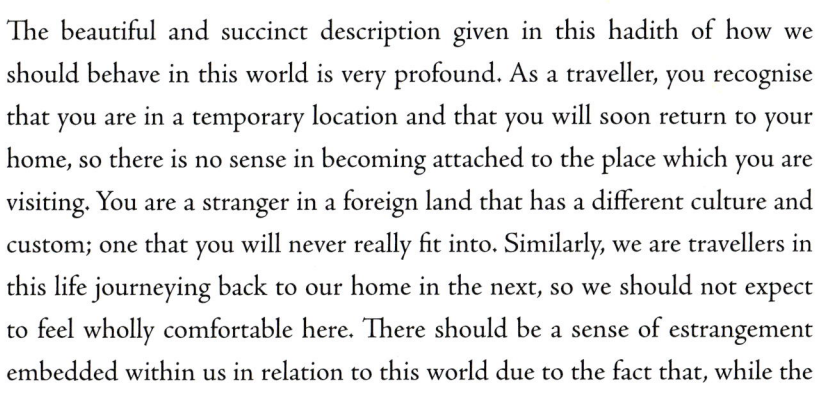

Be in this world as if you were a stranger or a traveller along a path.
(Sahih Bukhari)

The beautiful and succinct description given in this hadith of how we should behave in this world is very profound. As a traveller, you recognise that you are in a temporary location and that you will soon return to your home, so there is no sense in becoming attached to the place which you are visiting. You are a stranger in a foreign land that has a different culture and custom; one that you will never really fit into. Similarly, we are travellers in this life journeying back to our home in the next, so we should not expect to feel wholly comfortable here. There should be a sense of estrangement embedded within us in relation to this world due to the fact that, while the world was created for us, we were not created for this world.

---

7 Imam Jalaludin, Abdur-Rahman ibn Abi Bakr Al-Suyuti, *Al-Durar Al-Munathati fi Al-Ahadith Al-Mashtahari* (Jamatul Malik Saud, Riyadh, 1979) p.197

Another analogy that has been given in regards to our relationship to this world is like that of a person sailing on the ocean to reach their destination. During the journey the person becomes thirsty and instead of waiting to reach their destination to quench their thirst, they decide to make a hole in the boat in order to obtain water to drink. Of course, the ocean water is salty so instead of quenching the person's thirst, it makes it worse. Meanwhile, the boat is slowly sinking and ultimately they drown in the ocean and fail either to quench their thirst or to make it to their destination.

The analogy of the ocean water is this dunya; we need it in order to reach the akhirah but it does not have the capacity to quench our inner longing for peace. The boat is the human heart, which so long as it uses the world as a means to the next life, it is healthy but when it becomes attached to this world, it will slowly drown in its deception. The destination, of course is paradise, which we are all striving to move towards. It is how we steer ourselves through the ocean that will determine our success in reaching our destination.

A prison

In this hadith, the world is described as a prison:

Abu Huraira ﷺ reported that the Messenger of Allah ﷺ said:
*The world is a prison for the believer
and a paradise for the unbeliever.*
(Sahih Muslim)

By the very nature of captivity, one can never be settled or content in a prison and in fact longs for freedom. For the believer, the world is similarly like a prison, in which they wait for the day they are free and able to return to paradise and to meet their Lord with the weight of good deeds weighing heavy on their scales.

A worthless thing

قَالَ كُنَّا مَعَ رَسُولِ اللَّهِ ﷺ بِذِى الْحُلَيْفَةِ فَإِذَا هُوَ بِشَاةٍ مَيِّتَةٍ شَائِلَةٍ بِرِجْلِهَا فَقَالَ أَتُرَوْنَ هَذِهِ هَيِّنَةً عَلَى صَاحِبِهَا فَوَالَّذِى نَفْسِى بِيَدِهِ لَلدُّنْيَا أَهْوَنُ عَلَى اللَّهِ مِنْ هَذِهِ عَلَى صَاحِبِهَا وَلَوْ كَانَتِ الدُّنْيَا تَزِنُ عِنْدَ اللَّهِ جَنَاحَ بَعُوضَةٍ مَا سَقَى كَافِرًا مِنْهَا قَطْرَةً أَبَدًا

It was narrated that Sahl ibn Sa'd ﷺ said:
We were with the Messenger of Allah ﷺ in Dhul-Hulaifah,
when we saw a dead sheep lifting its leg (because of bloating).
He said: "Don't you think this is worthless to its owner?
By the One in Whose hand is my soul, this world is more
worthless to Allah than this (dead sheep) is to its owner.
If this world was worth the wing of a mosquito to Allah,
the disbeliever would not have a drop to drink from it."
(Sunan Ibn Majah)

What an apt analogy from the Prophet Muhammad ﷺ! The world has less value than the wing of a mosquito and is more worthless than a rotting carcass. How, after realising the true nature of this world, can we still prefer it to the next life?

During the time of the 'Abbasid caliphate, a wealthy and expansive empire, Ibn al-Sammak, a skilled rhetorician and speech writer, visited the Caliph, Harun ar-Rashid. The caliph began to feel thirsty and requested water to drink. Ibn al-Sammak asked the caliph if he was denied a drink of water, would he give half his kingdom in return for a drink? The caliph answered in the affirmative; that he would indeed give up half his kingdom for a drink of water. We know that water is essential for human survival and without access to it, a person will die within days. Then Ibn al-Sammak asked the caliph if due to some sickness, he was not able to discharge the water he drank (i.e. through urine), would he give half of his empire to be able to discharge it? Again, the caliph answered in the affirmative. Again we know if a person loses their ability to pass water, this is a most painful condition and can lead to death. Ibn al-Sammak then turned to Harun ar-Rashid and said: "Therefore, there is no good in a kingdom that is not even equal to a drink of water."[8]

A cursed delusion

In another hadith this world is not only described in a lowly manner but is said to be cursed:

أَلَا إِنَّ الدُّنْيَا مَلْعُونَةٌ مَلْعُونٌ مَا فِيهَا إِلَّا ذِكْرُ اللَّهِ وَمَا وَالَاهُ وَعَالِمٌ أَوْ مُتَعَلِّمٌ

Abu Huraira ﷺ reported that the Messenger of Allah ﷺ said:
Is not the world cursed and everything in it?
Except for the remembrance of Allah and what facilitates it,
the scholar or the student.
(Sunan al-Tirmidhi)

---

8 Cited by Al-Qarni, trans. Faisal ibn Muhammad Shafeeq, *Don't be Sad* (International Islamic Publishing House, Riyadh, 2005) p.154

How unfortunate is the one who chases after something that is cursed? Not only is this world lowly, worthless and accursed but it is a place that will deceive and make you forget the true nature of your existence. Allah ﷻ says in the Qur'an:

ٱعْلَمُوٓا۟ أَنَّمَا ٱلْحَيَوٰةُ ٱلدُّنْيَا لَعِبٌ وَلَهْوٌ وَزِينَةٌ وَتَفَاخُرٌۢ بَيْنَكُمْ وَتَكَاثُرٌ فِى ٱلْأَمْوَٰلِ وَٱلْأَوْلَٰدِ كَمَثَلِ غَيْثٍ أَعْجَبَ ٱلْكُفَّارَ نَبَاتُهُۥ ثُمَّ يَهِيجُ فَتَرَىٰهُ مُصْفَرًّا ثُمَّ يَكُونُ حُطَٰمًا وَفِى ٱلْءَاخِرَةِ عَذَابٌ شَدِيدٌ وَمَغْفِرَةٌ مِّنَ ٱللَّهِ وَرِضْوَٰنٌ وَمَا ٱلْحَيَوٰةُ ٱلدُّنْيَآ إِلَّا مَتَٰعُ ٱلْغُرُورِ

Know that the life of this world is merely a game and a diversion and ostentation and a cause of boasting among yourselves and trying to outdo one another in wealth and children: like the plant growth after rain which delights the cultivators, but then it withers and you see it turning yellow and then it becomes broken stubble. In the Next World there is terrible punishment but also forgiveness from Allah and His good pleasure. The life of this world is nothing but the enjoyment of delusion.
(Surah al-Hadid 57:20)

Amusement, diversion, adornment, mutual boasting and competition for wealth and children – this is what life ultimately means to the people of this world. They busy themselves with play and entertainment; they seek to adorn themselves and chase after the material adornments of this world. When they achieve some status or position or material gain in life, they boast about it and ultimately they compete in accumulation of wealth and having their progeny carry on their legacy. Yet all the play, entertainment, material objects, social status, wealth and children that a person occupied their whole life in acquiring, will reduce to nothing just as vegetation withers away and becomes stubble with the coming of the next season. In our case, our next season is our death, while this one is simply an *enjoyment of delusion*.

Chasing a shadow

The Prophet ﷺ has given excellent advice in the following hadith:

مَنْ كَانَتْ الدُّنْيَا هَمَّهُ فَرَّقَ اللَّهُ عَلَيْهِ أَمْرَهُ وَجَعَلَ فَقْرَهُ بَيْنَ عَيْنَيْهِ وَلَمْ يَأْتِهِ مِنْ الدُّنْيَا إِلَّا مَا كُتِبَ لَهُ وَمَنْ كَانَتْ الْآخِرَةُ نِيَّتَهُ جَمَعَ اللَّهُ لَهُ أَمْرَهُ وَجَعَلَ غِنَاهُ فِي قَلْبِهِ وَأَتَتْهُ الدُّنْيَا وَهِيَ رَاغِمَةٌ

Zayd ibn Thabit ؓ reported that the Messenger of Allah ﷺ said:
Whoever makes the world his most important matter,
Allah will confound his affairs and make poverty appear before
his eyes and he will not get anything from the world but what has
been decreed for him. Whoever makes the Hereafter his most important matter,
Allah will settle his affairs and make him content in his heart and the
world will come to him although he does not want it.
(Sunan Ibn Majah)

When you make the world your primary concern you will become impoverished, whatever the extent of your wealth, luxuries and material gains. We see this in the modern world, particularly in the developed nations, that the majority have access to what would have been considered luxuries in the past, such as running water, abundance of food, ability to travel the world at rapid speed, access to unlimited information at our fingertips and yet we are still impoverished. We are still seeking the path to peace; we are still seeking to find something more substantial as evidenced by the rise of interest in therapy or meditation or retreats in the West. Clearly, material wealth is not proving to be enough to be content.

By its very nature, the more you chase this dunya the more it will evade you. Just as you will never catch your shadow no matter how fast you chase it. However, if you turn your back to your shadow and run towards the source of light – the sun – your shadow will follow you. So in the same way, when you run towards Allah ﷻ, the Light of the Heavens and Earth, the world will come running under your feet without you even wanting it!

ٱللَّهُ نُورُ ٱلسَّمَٰوَٰتِ وَٱلْأَرْضِ ۚ مَثَلُ نُورِهِۦ كَمِشْكَوٰةٍ فِيهَا مِصْبَاحٌ ۖ ٱلْمِصْبَاحُ فِى زُجَاجَةٍ ۖ ٱلزُّجَاجَةُ كَأَنَّهَا كَوْكَبٌ دُرِّىٌّ يُوقَدُ مِن شَجَرَةٍ مُّبَٰرَكَةٍ زَيْتُونَةٍ لَّا شَرْقِيَّةٍ وَلَا غَرْبِيَّةٍ يَكَادُ زَيْتُهَا يُضِىٓءُ وَلَوْ لَمْ تَمْسَسْهُ نَارٌ ۚ نُّورٌ عَلَىٰ نُورٍ ۗ يَهْدِى ٱللَّهُ لِنُورِهِۦ مَن يَشَآءُ ۚ وَيَضْرِبُ ٱللَّهُ ٱلْأَمْثَٰلَ لِلنَّاسِ ۗ وَٱللَّهُ بِكُلِّ شَىْءٍ عَلِيمٌ

Allah is the Light of the heavens and earth, the metaphor of His Light is that of a niche in which is a lamp, the lamp inside a glass, the glass like a brilliant star, lit from a blessed tree, an olive, neither of the east nor of the west, its oil all but giving off light even if no fire touches it, Light upon Light, Allah guides to His Light whomever He wills and Allah makes metaphors for mankind and Allah has knowledge of all things.

(Surah an-Nur 24:35)

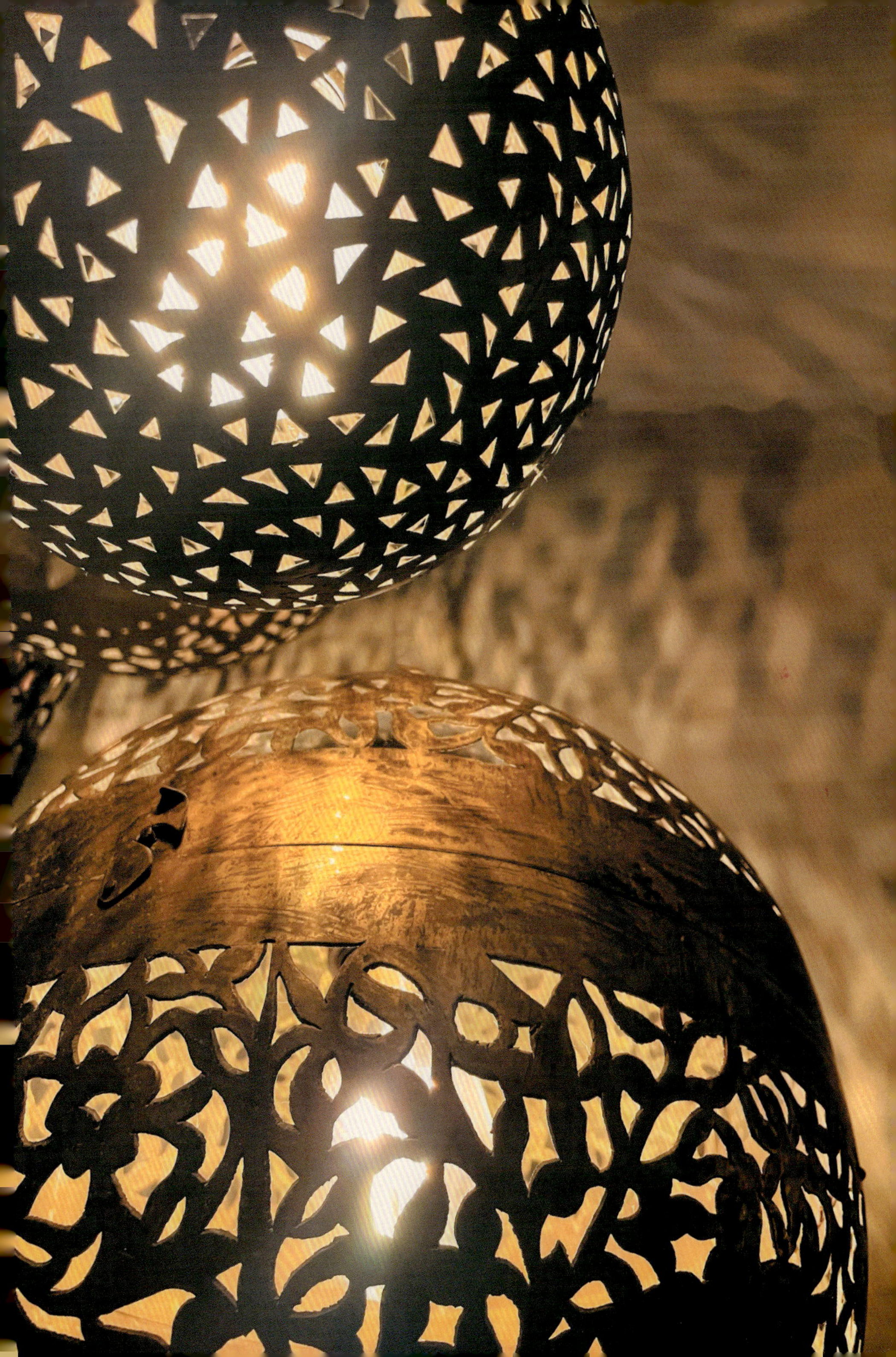

Names and Qualities of Allah ﷻ

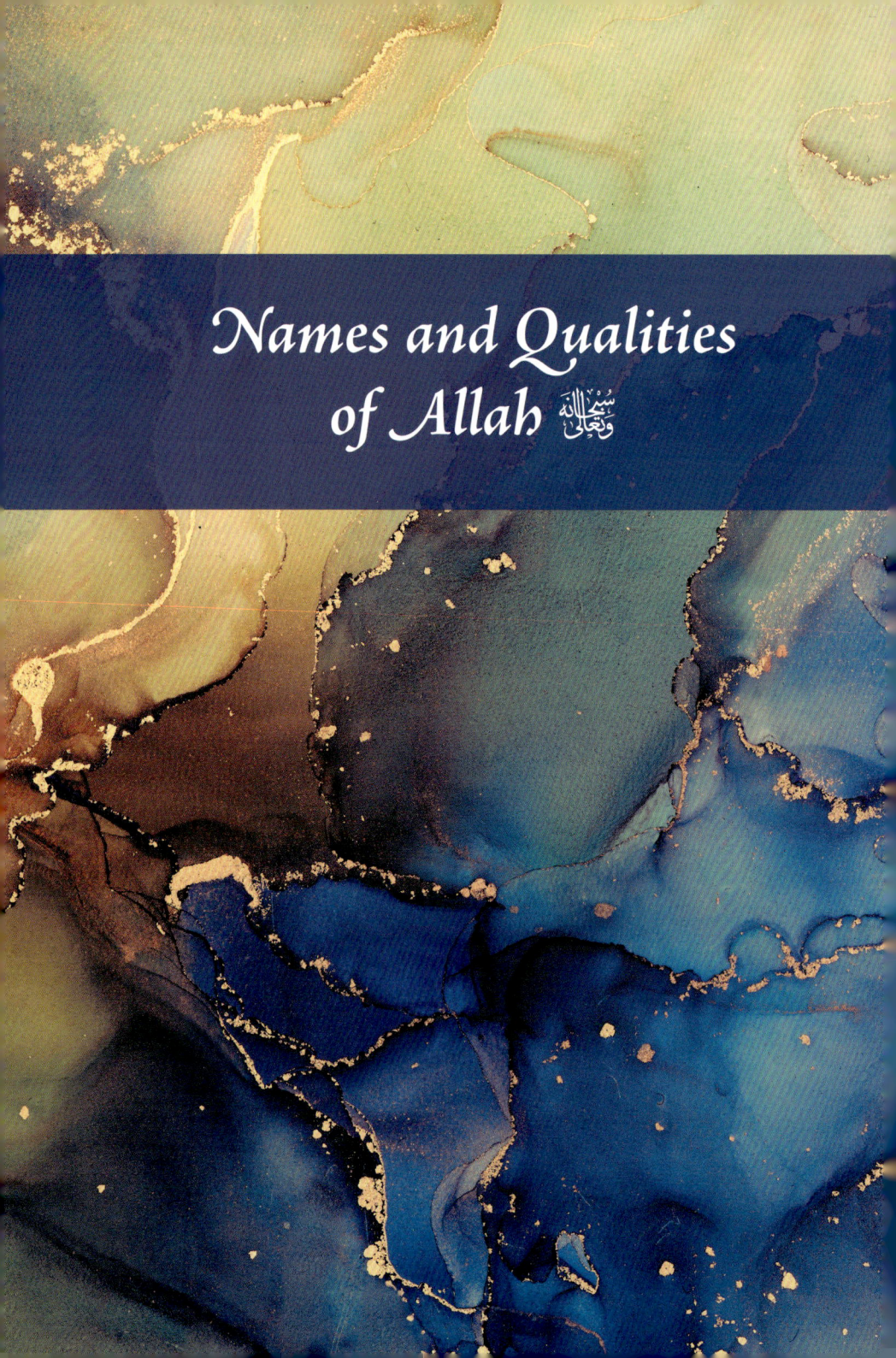

If God is All-Powerful and All-Merciful then why does He allow evil to happen?

This is the famous question that is used by atheists to attack the idea of God and by extension, the beliefs that come with belief in God, such the afterlife. A good starting point for answering this question would be to define evil. Is evil something relative to how we perceive existence, or does it have a reality of its own?

As beings with finite limits as to how our mind functions, we only have a partial understanding of the nature of reality in line with what we can perceive. Therefore what might appear to be evil from our limited perception of existence may not be evil within the context of the complete nature of reality. A tiny ant crawling on an open book will only be able to perceive the ink of some letters on a page and will not have the capacity to see and understand the totality of the entire book. Human beings are in a similar situation where can see glimpses of the world using our limited and finite senses and understanding, but the vastness of creation is too great for our minds to encompass completely.

Another aspect of the question that needs to be addressed in further depth is the concept of God. Allah ﷻ will always remain incomprehensible to the human mind but He ﷻ does have names and attributes through which we can better understand Him ﷻ. And once we can begin to understand the concept of Allah ﷻ, we can gain a better understanding of the grand scale of existence and how human suffering fits within this broader picture of reality. Here are just a few attributes of Allah to help in starting to build that understanding.

The All-Knowing

اَلْعَلِيمُ

وَعَسَىٰ أَن تَكْرَهُوا شَيْئًا وَهُوَ خَيْرٌ لَّكُمْ ۖ وَعَسَىٰ أَن تُحِبُّوا شَيْئًا وَهُوَ شَرٌّ لَّكُمْ ۗ وَاللَّهُ يَعْلَمُ وَأَنتُمْ لَا تَعْلَمُونَ

It may be that you hate something when it is good for you and it may be that you love something when it is bad for you. Allah knows and you do not know.
(Surah al-Baqarah 2:216)

Allah ﷻ knows what is better for us in the long term. When a child is suffering from illness, her parents may need to administer bitter tasting medicine, may need to wake the sleeping child, may need to take her to a doctor. Parents do this despite the cries and tears of the child because they realise that it is in the greater interest of the child to be restored to good health, by the will of Allah ﷻ. The pain of the medication and discomfort of the doctor's office are temporary nuisances in order to realise the greater long term benefits.

Similarly, Allah ﷻ will allow us to go through things in life that we may find painful. We may resist and shed tears and complain, but this is a necessary process for our own spiritual betterment and growth.

One example of Allah's ﷻ attribute of Al-'Aleem, The All-Knowing, becoming manifest in the life of the Prophet ﷺ was at the Treaty of Hudaybiyyah in the 6th year of Hijrah. The Prophet Muhammad ﷺ and a group of Muslims had come from Madinah to Makkah in order to perform 'Umrah but they were stopped at Hudaybiyyah by the Makkan Quraysh. After lengthy negotiations, a treaty was signed in which the Muslims had to make a number of concessions and were not allowed to perform the 'Umrah until the following year. The Sahabah were very grieved at this, as this seemed to be the ultimate humiliation for the Muslims following years of persecution at the hands of the Quraysh.

The Muslims returned heavy hearted but on the way back to Makkah, the following ayat were revealed:

إِنَّا فَتَحْنَا لَكَ فَتْحًا مُّبِينًا لِّيَغْفِرَ لَكَ ٱللَّهُ مَا تَقَدَّمَ مِن ذَنۢبِكَ وَمَا تَأَخَّرَ وَيُتِمَّ نِعْمَتَهُۥ عَلَيْكَ وَيَهْدِيَكَ صِرَٰطًا مُّسْتَقِيمًا وَيَنصُرَكَ ٱللَّهُ نَصْرًا عَزِيزًا

Truly We have granted you a clear victory so that Allah may forgive you your earlier errors and any later ones and complete His blessing upon you, and guide you on a Straight Path, and so that Allah may help you with a mighty help.
(Surah al-Fath 48:1-3)

At the time, no one understood how this could have been a victory. However, the fullness of time showed that it was the Treaty of Hudaybiyyah that paved the way for Islam to be accepted in masses across the Arabian Peninsula and to the eventual Opening of Makkah, all without bloodshed or destruction.

Another incident in Islamic history that illustrates the limits of human knowledge in relation to the Infinite and All-Encompassing knowledge of Allah ﷻ can be seen in the encounter of Musa ﷺ with Khidr ﷺ, as recounted in Surah al-Kahf. According to some scholars Khidr ﷺ was a prophet while others maintain he was someone very close to Allah ﷻ. Yet the combined knowledge of these great men was incomparable to the vastness of Allah's ﷻ knowledge.

فَنَقَرَ نَقْرَةً أَوْ نَقْرَتَيْنِ فِي الْبَحْرِ فَقَالَ الْخَضِرُ يَا مُوسَى مَا نَقَصَ عِلْمِي وَعِلْمُكَ مِنْ عِلْمِ اللَّهِ إِلَّا كَنَقْرَةِ هَذَا الْعُصْفُورِ فِي الْبَحْرِ

Ubayy ibn Ka'b ﷺ reported that the Messenger of Allah ﷺ said:
...Then a sparrow came and stood on the edge of the boat and dipped its beak once or twice in the sea. Al-Khidr said: "O Musa! My knowledge and your knowledge have not decreased Allah's knowledge except as much as this sparrow has decreased the water of the sea with its beak."...
(part of a longer hadith in Sahih Bukhari)

This serves for us to understand that if we accept our limits of knowledge, then it is easier to accept and be content with whatever comes our way in life. So we trust in this attribute of Allah ﷻ, that He ﷻ knows what is best for us while we do not know. He ﷻ knows our future and how the path of our past and present connects to the future and He ﷻ will seamlessly guide us through that path because He ﷻ is the All-Knowing.

The Most Generous

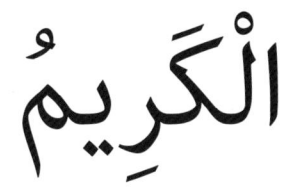

$$\text{ٱلْكَرِيمُ}$$

There are times in life that we experience such great loss as to shake our iman (faith) and it is at precisely these times that it is important to recognise that Allah ﷻ is Al-Kareem, The Most Generous. What may appear to be a loss is actually a means of protecting us from a greater calamity or of increasing us in a blessing later in life.

Continuing with the story of Musa ﷺ and Khidr ﷺ, Surah al-Kahf relates how they both travelled on a boat as guests when Khidr ﷺ made a hole in the boat. Musa ﷺ questioned this act of Khidr ﷺ damaging the boat of the very people that had offered them a ride. Khidr ﷺ explained later in the surah that he had damaged the boat as a command from Allah ﷻ to protect them from a king who was seizing all boats that were in good condition. What appeared to be a loss for the boatmen was in reality a means of protecting them from the greater loss of having their ship seized by the king.

$$\text{أَمَّا ٱلسَّفِينَةُ فَكَانَتْ لِمَسَٰكِينَ يَعْمَلُونَ فِى ٱلْبَحْرِ فَأَرَدتُّ أَنْ أَعِيبَهَا وَكَانَ وَرَآءَهُم مَّلِكٌ يَأْخُذُ كُلَّ سَفِينَةٍ غَصْبًا}$$

As for the boat, it belonged to some poor people who worked on the sea. I wanted to damage it because a king was coming behind them, commandeering every boat.
(Surah al-Kahf 18:79)

Sufyan At-Thawri once stated regarding Allah's wisdom in allowing us to experience loss:

> *Verily, when He withholds, He actually gives, because He did not withhold on account of miserliness or stinginess, but rather He looked at the benefit of His believing servant. So the fact that He withheld is actually His choice (for the servant) and His excellent decision.*[9]

---

[9] Ibn Qayyim, Madarij as-Saliheen, 2/176 cited in Aisha Utz, *The Prick of a Thorn* (International Islamic Publishing House, Riyadh, 2014) p.173

And further:

إِنَّ اللَّهَ تَعَالَى قَسَمَ بَيْنَكُمْ أَخْلاَقَكُمْ كَمَا قَسَمَ بَيْنَكُمْ أَرْزَاقَكُمْ وَإِنَّ اللَّهَ تَعَالَى يُعْطِي الْمَالَ مَنْ أَحَبَّ وَمَنْ لاَ يُحِبُّ وَلاَ يُعْطِي الإِيمَانَ إِلاَّ مَنْ يُحِبُّ فَمَنْ ضَنَّ بِالْمَالِ أَنْ يُنْفِقَهُ وَخَافَ الْعَدُوَّ أَنْ يُجَاهِدَهُ وَهَابَ اللَّيْلَ أَنْ يُكَابِدَهُ فَلْيُكْثِرْ مِنْ قَوْلِ لاَ إِلَهَ إِلاَّ اللَّهُ وَسُبْحَانَ اللَّهِ وَالْحَمْدُ لِلَّهِ وَاللَّهُ أَكْبَرُ

Abdullah ibn Mas'ud ﷺ said:
Allah Almighty allotted character between you as
He divided provision between you.
Allah Almighty bestows wealth on those He loves and those
He does not love. He only bestows faith upon those whom He loves.
Whoever is stingy about spending his wealth,
fears to fight the enemy, and is terrified of enduring the night
should frequently repeat, "There is no god worthy of
worship but Allah, Glory be to Allah, All praises are due to Allah,
and Allah is the greatest."
(Adab al-Mufrad)

Therefore, no matter what loss we have experienced in life, we have as believers the greatest gift of all, which is iman. No tragedy or loss can ever take away the fact that we have been chosen by Allah ﷻ to be gifted with this most precious gift of iman, out of His ﷻ Generosity towards us. After all, wealth and luxuries can be given to anyone. The Qur'an is filled with examples of extremely wealthy and influential men in their respective societies, such as Fir'awn, Abu Lahab and Abu Jahal, yet they were not gifted with iman and so, not only has all that wealth and power been reduced to nothing, they are forever remembered as earning the wrath of Allah ﷻ.

From this we understand that whatever Allah has bestowed upon us or withheld from us is from His Generosity and the most generous gift that He has blessed us with is iman. One of the recommended daily du'a is:

$$\text{رَضِيتُ بِاللَّهِ رَبًّا وَبِالإِسْلَامِ دِينًا وَبِمُحَمَّدٍ نَبِيًّا}$$

Radeetu billāhi Rabban wa bil Islāmi dinan wa bi Muhammadin nabīyyan

I am pleased with Allah as my Lord,
Islam as my religion and
Muhammad as my Prophet.
(Sunan Ibn Majah)[10]

This du'a provides us with a very powerful daily reminder that even if we have nothing in material terms in this world, so long as we have Allah as our Lord, Muhammad as our Prophet and Islam as our religion, the reality is that we have the most valuable blessings of all.

---

10 The full hadith is: Abu Salam reported that the Messenger of Allah said: *There is no Muslim - or no person, or slave (of Allah) - who says, in the morning and evening: Radeetu billāhi Rabban wa bil Islāmi dinan wa bi Muhammadin nabiyyan (I am pleased with Allah as my Lord, Islam as my religion and Muhammad as my Prophet), but he will have a promise from Allah to make him pleased on the Day of Resurrection.* (Sunan Ibn Majah)

The Omnipotent

$$\text{الْقَادِرُ}$$

Whatever trial or tribulation we find ourselves going through, we should recognise that it could not have occurred without the will of Allah ﷻ. The same applies to every ease and abundance that we are granted. Therefore, we should not grieve at every sorrow nor become complacent at every blessing. We should recognise that there is not a trial in this world but that it can turn into a blessing and there is not a blessing but that it can turn into a trial; for if a trial becomes a means of us getting closer to Allah ﷻ then in reality it was a blessing and if a blessing is a means of us becoming distant from Allah ﷻ then in reality it was a trial. Everything has been written and will come to pass and we should remain steadfast and constant in our remembrance of Allah ﷻ throughout it all.

مَا أَصَابَ مِن مُّصِيبَةٍ فِي الْأَرْضِ وَلَا فِي أَنفُسِكُمْ إِلَّا فِي كِتَابٍ مِّن قَبْلِ أَن نَّبْرَأَهَا ۚ إِنَّ ذَٰلِكَ عَلَى اللَّهِ يَسِيرٌ لِّكَيْلَا تَأْسَوْا عَلَىٰ مَا فَاتَكُمْ وَلَا تَفْرَحُوا بِمَا آتَاكُمْ ۗ وَاللَّهُ لَا يُحِبُّ كُلَّ مُخْتَالٍ فَخُورٍ

Nothing occurs, either in the earth or in yourselves, without its being in a Book before We make it happen. That is something easy for Allah. That is so that you will not be grieved about the things that pass you by or exult about the things that come to you. Allah does not love any vain or boastful man.

(Surah al-Hadid 57:22-23)

Whatever it is that we are going through comes only from Allah ﷺ and it is only Allah ﷺ that can bring about change to the situation.

كُنْتُ خَلْفَ رَسُولِ اللَّهِ ﷺ يَوْمًا فَقَالَ يَا غُلَامُ إِنِّي أُعَلِّمُكَ كَلِمَاتٍ احْفَظِ اللَّهَ يَحْفَظْكَ احْفَظِ اللَّهَ تَجِدْهُ تُجَاهَكَ إِذَا سَأَلْتَ فَاسْأَلِ اللَّهَ وَإِذَا اسْتَعَنْتَ فَاسْتَعِنْ بِاللَّهِ وَاعْلَمْ أَنَّ الْأُمَّةَ لَوِ اجْتَمَعَتْ عَلَى أَنْ يَنْفَعُوكَ بِشَيْءٍ لَمْ يَنْفَعُوكَ إِلَّا بِشَيْءٍ قَدْ كَتَبَهُ اللَّهُ لَكَ وَإِنِ اجْتَمَعُوا عَلَى أَنْ يَضُرُّوكَ بِشَيْءٍ لَمْ يَضُرُّوكَ إِلَّا بِشَيْءٍ قَدْ كَتَبَهُ اللَّهُ عَلَيْكَ رُفِعَتِ الْأَقْلَامُ وَجَفَّتِ الصُّحُفُ

Ibn 'Abbas ﴾ reported: One day I was behind the Prophet ﷺ [riding on the same mount] and he said,
O young man, I shall teach you some words [of advice]: Be mindful of Allah and Allah will protect you. Be mindful of Allah and you will find Him in front of you. If you ask, then ask Allah [alone]; and if you seek help, then seek help from Allah [alone]. And know that if the nation were to gather together to benefit you with anything, they would not benefit you except with what Allah had already prescribed for you. And if they were to gather together to harm you with anything, they would not harm you except with what Allah had already prescribed against you. The pens have been lifted and the pages have dried.
(Sunan at-Tirmidhi)

From this, we learn to be always mindful of Allah ﷺ; to turn to Him ﷺ alone in times of ease and in times of trouble. There is nothing in the world that can help us if Allah ﷺ is not on our side and there is nothing in the world that can harm us if Allah ﷺ is with us. He ﷺ is Al-Qadir, The Omnipotent.

The Most Merciful, The Most Compassionate

الرَّحْمَنُ الرَّحِيمُ

Two of the most repeated names of Allah ﷻ in the Qur'an are Ar-Rahman and Ar-Raheem, The Most Merciful and The Most Compassionate, so much so that these names are at the start of every surah in the Qur'an except Surah at-Tawbah. When we think about compassion and mercy, the relationship that shows the epitome of these qualities in the human realm is that of a mother towards her child, yet this hadith explains that Allah ﷻ is far more merciful to us than even our own mothers.

قَدِمَ عَلَى النَّبِيِّ ﷺ سَبْيٌ فَإِذَا امْرَأَةٌ مِنَ السَّبْيِ قَدْ تَحْلُبُ ثَدْيَهَا تَسْقِي إِذَا وَجَدَتْ صَبِيًّا فِي السَّبْيِ أَخَذَتْهُ فَأَلْصَقَتْهُ بِبَطْنِهَا وَأَرْضَعَتْهُ فَقَالَ لَنَا النَّبِيُّ ﷺ أَتُرَوْنَ هَذِهِ طَارِحَةً وَلَدَهَا فِي النَّارِ قُلْنَا لَا وَهِيَ تَقْدِرُ عَلَى أَنْ لَا تَطْرَحَهُ فَقَالَ لَلَّهُ أَرْحَمُ بِعِبَادِهِ مِنْ هَذِهِ بِوَلَدِهَا

'Umar ibn al-Khattab ؓ reported:
Some prisoners of war were brought to the Prophet ﷺ and a breastfeeding woman was among them. Whenever she found a child among the prisoners, she would take it to her chest and nurse it. The Prophet ﷺ said to us, "Do you think this woman would throw her child in the fire?" We said, "No, not if she was able to stop it." The Prophet ﷺ said, "Allah is more merciful to his servants than a mother is to her child."
(Sahih Bukhari and Muslim)

In fact, all the mercy we see in this world is only one percent of the mercy of Allah ﷺ:

> إِنَّ اللَّهَ خَلَقَ يَوْمَ خَلَقَ السَّمَاوَاتِ وَالْأَرْضَ مِائَةَ رَحْمَةٍ كُلُّ رَحْمَةٍ طِبَاقَ مَا بَيْنَ السَّمَاءِ وَالْأَرْضِ فَجَعَلَ مِنْهَا فِي الْأَرْضِ رَحْمَةً فَبِهَا تَعْطِفُ الْوَالِدَةُ عَلَى وَلَدِهَا وَالْوَحْشُ وَالطَّيْرُ بَعْضُهَا عَلَى بَعْضٍ فَإِذَا كَانَ يَوْمُ الْقِيَامَةِ أَكْمَلَهَا بِهَذِهِ الرَّحْمَةِ

Salman al-Farsi ؓ reported that the Messenger of Allah ﷺ said: *Verily, on the day Allah created the heavens and earth, He created one hundred parts of mercy. Each part can fill what is between the heaven and earth. He made one part of mercy for the earth, from it a mother has compassion for her child, animals and birds have compassion for each other. On the Day of Resurrection, He will perfect this mercy.*
(Sahih Muslim)

The word in Arabic for womb, the protected shelter in which we start our life on earth and in which all our needs are supplied, is الرَّحِم and has the same root from which الرَّحْمَٰن and الرَّحِيم are derived.

> إِنَّ الرَّحِمَ شَجْنَةٌ مِنَ الرَّحْمَٰنِ فَقَالَ اللهُ مَنْ وَصَلَكِ وَصَلْتُهُ وَمَنْ قَطَعَكِ قَطَعْتُهُ

Abu Huraira ؓ reported that the Prophet ﷺ said: *Verily, the womb derives its name from the Most Merciful. Allah said: I will keep good relations with one who keeps good relations with your relatives, and I will sever relations with one who severs relations with your relatives.*
(Sahih Bukhari)

When we begin to comprehend the extent of Allah's mercy towards us, then it is easier to move through difficult times with confidence and reassurance that Allah is The Most Compassionate and The Most Merciful towards us and every situation that we find ourselves in is as a result of that infinite mercy.

The Most Loving

الْوَدُودُ

Finally we look at the quality of Allah that is Al-Wadud, The Most Loving. There is no entity that can and does love us more than Allah. The name Al-Wadud only occurs in the Qur'an twice:

وَاسْتَغْفِرُوا رَبَّكُمْ ثُمَّ تُوبُوا إِلَيْهِ إِنَّ رَبِّي رَحِيمٌ وَدُودٌ

Ask your Lord for forgiveness and then turn in repentance to Him. My Lord is most Merciful, Most Loving.
(Surah Hud 11:90)

In this case, we are instructed in clear terms how we can access Allah's ﷻ mercy and love and that is through seeking forgiveness and repentance. The second occurrence is:

$$\text{وَهُوَ ٱلْغَفُورُ ٱلْوَدُودُ}$$

He is the Ever-Forgiving, the All-Loving.
(Surah al-Buruj 85:14)

Surah al-Buruj speaks of the persecution of the believers on the basis of their faith. This is the ultimate trial that any believer can undergo and yet in the face of this immense suffering, Allah ﷻ reveals He ﷻ is The Most Loving. This is a reminder for us that in our darkest hours and most difficult circumstances Allah ﷻ has not forsaken us nor does He ﷻ hate us. It is in these very words that Allah ﷻ Himself consoled the Prophet ﷺ.

$$\text{مَا وَدَّعَكَ رَبُّكَ وَمَا قَلَىٰ}$$

Your Lord has not abandoned you nor does He hate you.
(Surah ad-Duha 93:3)

It was in the early days of Islam and the Prophet ﷺ had stopped receiving Qur'anic revelation for a period. The unbelievers taunted him and this caused great anxiety for the Prophet ﷺ who felt that Allah ﷻ had abandoned him. So Allah ﷻ revealed Surah ad-Duha to comfort the Prophet ﷺ directly.

The word for love that appears in the Qur'an most often is الحب, while the name Al-Wadud derives from the word الود. The latter is a stronger term for love and carries the additional sense of manifesting that love by giving. So Allah's ﷻ being Al-Wadud is not just a passive feeling on His ﷻ part but it carries the sense that He ﷻ will express that love through giving.

This is just a glimpse into the concept of Allah and from this we can see that it is us humans who are limited in our imagination and shackled by anxiety because Allah's ﷻ mercy, knowledge, power, compassion and love are all far in excess of what we can imagine and He ﷻ Himself has frequently told us of His ﷻ attributes through the Qur'an and hadith so that we can be reassured.

Benefits of
Trials and Tribulations

When we want to advance in life, whether that be in school or our careers, one of the means through which to do this is to undergo examinations. The exams that we take will often be challenging and we will have to undergo hardship to prepare for them and sacrifice our free time or other leisure activities. However, we are prepared to do all this because we have a goal in mind and we want to achieve it in order to enjoy the success that brings, be it titles, respect, increased salary, promotion and so on. As we move higher in our education and career, the exams become increasingly more challenging so as to separate the best in the field from the others. In a similar manner, we undergo trials and tribulations in order to achieve excellence in the hereafter, which is our goal for success. When this is clear, then it becomes much easier to be consistent in dealing with them and to make sacrifices along the path of life in order to reach the heights of our spiritual development. There are a number of benefits to patiently dealing with hardship.

Your sins will be removed

مَا يُصِيبُ الْمُسْلِمَ مِنْ نَصَبٍ وَلاَ وَصَبٍ وَلاَ هَمٍّ وَلاَ حُزْنٍ وَلاَ أَذًى وَلاَ غَمٍّ حَتَّى الشَّوْكَةِ يُشَاكُهَا إِلاَّ كَفَّرَ اللَّهُ بِهَا مِنْ خَطَايَاهُ

Abu Sa'id al-Khudri ☺ and Abu Huraira ☺ reported that the Messenger of Allah ﷺ said:
No fatigue, nor disease, nor sorrow, nor sadness, nor hurt, nor distress befalls a Muslim, even if it were the prick he receives from a thorn, but that Allah expiates some of his sins for that.
(Sahih Bukhari)

How beautiful is it that Allah ﷻ will remove our sins for every hardship we go through even if it be the most minute difficulty; each pricking of a thorn will be a means by which our sins burn away? The expiation of sins through difficulty occurs to the extent that some people will have all their sins removed because of the hardships they endured.

الْبَلَاءُ بِالْعَبْدِ حَتَّى يَتْرُكَهُ يَمْشِى عَلَى الْأَرْضِ مَا عَلَيْهِ خَطِيئَةٌ

Mus'ad ibn Sa'id ☺ reported that the Messenger of Allah ﷺ said:
The servant will continue to be tried until he is left walking upon the earth without any sin.
(Sunan at-Tirmidhi)

Your heart will be guided and purified by Allah ﷻ

Allah ﷻ has promised He ﷻ will guide the heart of the one who believes.

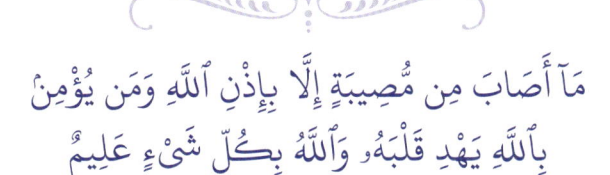

مَآ أَصَابَ مِن مُّصِيبَةٍ إِلَّا بِإِذْنِ ٱللَّهِ وَمَن يُؤْمِنۢ بِٱللَّهِ يَهْدِ قَلْبَهُۥ وَٱللَّهُ بِكُلِّ شَىْءٍ عَلِيمٌ

No misfortune occurs except by Allah's permission. Whoever believes in Allah – He will guide his heart. Allah has knowledge of all things.
(Surah at-Taghabun 64:11)

The heart, by its very nature, is unstable and constantly fluctuating as Abu Musa ؓ reported that the Prophet ﷺ said:

مَثَلُ الْقَلْبِ مَثَلُ الرِّيشَةِ تُقَلِّبُهَا الرِّيَاحُ بِفَلَاةٍ

The parable of the heart is that of a feather blown about by the wind of the desert.
(Sunan Ibn Majah)

The unstable nature of the heart is embedded in the Arabic word for heart itself. The verb qalaba – قَلَبَ – means 'to convert, transform, turn, change, alter'.[11] The Prophet ﷺ further explained this by stating:

$$\text{إِنَّمَا سُمِّيَ الْقَلْبُ مِنْ تَقَلُّبِهِ}$$

Verily, it is only called the heart because it fluctuates.
(Sunan Ibn Majah)

Through the storms of a trial, the heart is liable to toss and turn with anxiety. However, if we have iman in Allah ﷻ, He ﷻ has promised He ﷻ will guide our ever-delicate heart, which had it not been for Allah's ﷻ protection, would be tossed about by the winds of temptation and trial. Not only will Allah ﷻ guide our heart, but through this process He ﷻ will also purify it:

$$\text{وَلِيَبْتَلِيَ ٱللَّهُ مَا فِى صُدُورِكُمْ وَلِيُمَحِّصَ مَا فِى قُلُوبِكُمْ وَٱللَّهُ عَلِيمٌۢ بِذَاتِ ٱلصُّدُورِ}$$

…So that Allah might test what is in your breasts and purge what is in your hearts. Allah know what your hearts contain…
(Surah Ali-Imran 3:154)

---

11 R. al-Baalbaki, *Al-Mawrid: A modern Arabic-English dictionary* (Dar Al-Ilm lil-Malayin, Beirut, 2007) p.870

This ayah was revealed regarding the Battle of Uhud where the believers suffered loss and were tested greatly by the attack of the Quraysh on them. Within this difficult situation Allah ﷻ revealed that they were tested so their hearts could be purified.

The trial will make you stronger

The main thing to remember about trials is that they are not designed to break us but rather to make us stronger. It is easy to fall into despair and negativity when we are faced with hardship. However, Allah ﷻ makes a beautiful promise that He ﷻ does not put a burden on any soul greater than it can bear. This is the first line of the last ayah of Surah al-Baqarah that is well-known and often recited:

لَا يُكَلِّفُ ٱللَّهُ نَفْسًا إِلَّا وُسْعَهَا

Allah does not impose on any self any more than it can stand...
(Surah al-Baqarah 2:286)

This fact alone should give us the confidence to realise that whatever situation we find ourselves in is proof that we can handle it. However much we feel that we cannot bear the hardship and are close to breaking point, the reality is that we can bear the trial. Not only do we have the strength to bear the trial, but the pain that we go through while dealing with hardship is what is making us stronger and transforms us for the better.

One analogy by which we can understand this is if you have a trainer who is helping you to improve the physical condition of your body. One of the means the trainer uses is to push you to your limit. You find yourself out of breath and sweating and experiencing muscle ache to complete the exercises. But this is the means to increase your stamina and improve your condition. Slowly your body gets stronger and you then go beyond the thresholds of physical fitness that you had even imagined you could achieve. That amazing feeling of achievement and satisfaction is not possible without coming out of the comfort zone to a place of difficulty, determination and hard work.

Allah ﷻ will put us in situations which we believe are too difficult for us but He ﷻ knows we can, not only handle that situation, but that it will be a means for us to become spiritually stronger and enjoy the rewards that that brings with it.

Another beautiful promise of Allah's ﷻ is that hardship does not come without ease:

فَإِنَّ مَعَ الْعُسْرِ يُسْرًا إِنَّ مَعَ الْعُسْرِ يُسْرًا

**For truly with hardship comes ease;
truly with hardship comes ease.**
(Surah ash-Sharh 94:5-6)

Ibn Kathir comments on the above ayah, "..*indeed the ease is found **with** the hardship*"[12], not just after it. From every trial there will be an opportunity of self-growth and development. The seeds of change and growth are implanted with every difficulty so that as you undergo a trial you are in the process of transformative change and spiritual understanding. A number of people who have been through the harshest trials of life often look back and credit their current success and transformation to that difficult period.

Allah ﷻ loves you

Amongst the most powerful virtues of trials is that when Allah ﷻ wants good for a person, He ﷻ will give him a trial and that trial in turn will be a means for that person to get closer to Allah ﷻ. Abu Huraira ؓ reported that the Messenger of Allah ﷺ said:

$$\text{مَنْ يُرِدِ اللَّهُ بِهِ خَيْرًا يُصِبْ مِنْهُ}$$

*If Allah intends good for someone,
then He afflicts him with trials.*
(Sahih Bukhari)

Based on this, we can understand that if a difficulty results in a person drawing closer to Allah ﷻ, then that difficulty was actually a blessing and not something evil since it became a means of achieving the greatest good, which is nearness to Allah ﷻ.

---

12 Ibn Kathir Dimashqi, *Tafsir Ibn Kathir* (Dar Al-Kotob Al-Ilmiyah, Beirut, 2012) Vol.4, p.457

Allah ﷻ is raising your status

As we have previously seen, the greatest gift that a person can get from a trial is nearness to Allah ﷻ and as one draws closer to Allah ﷻ, they will be raised in spiritual status. Allah ﷻ has decreed the status of His servants and if Allah ﷻ wishes for someone to live up to that status, then He ﷻ will send trials upon them to raise them up.

إِنَّ الْعَبْدَ إِذَا سَبَقَتْ لَهُ مِنَ اللَّهِ مَنْزِلَةٌ لَمْ يَبْلُغْهَا بِعَمَلِهِ ابْتَلَاهُ اللَّهُ فِي جَسَدِهِ أَوْ فِي مَالِهِ أَوْ فِي وَلَدِهِ

Muhammad ibn Khalid as-Sulami narrated on his father's authority that his grandfather reported: He was a Companion of the Messenger of Allah said: I heard the Messenger of Allah say:
When Allah has previously decreed for a servant a rank which he has not attained by his action, He afflicts him in his body, or his property or his children.
(Sunan Abu Dawud)

We can see from the lives of many righteous people that this raise in status may not only apply to the hereafter but also to this life as well. We can see this in the life of Bilal ibn Rabah ؓ, whose master was displeased that his slave had accepted Islam. He tortured Bilal ؓ by placing a boulder on his chest in the burning daytime heat of the desert. Bilal ؓ would only cry 'Ahad - One'. If Bilal ؓ had just uttered a word of disbelief, then the torture would have stopped – and statements of disbelief under duress are permitted within Islam. Nevertheless, Bilal ؓ remained steadfast and continued to declare the Oneness of Allah ﷻ. At that time, Abu Bakr ﷺ bought Bilal ﷺ and the torture stopped. Years later that same melodious voice that proclaimed tawheed (Oneness of Allah) in the midst of immense torture and difficulty, was chosen by the Prophet ﷺ himself to be the first mu'adhdhin (caller to prayer) in Islamic history and, at the Opening of Makkah, proclaimed the adhan from the roof of the Ka'bah in front of thousands. This is the very Companion about whom the Prophet ﷺ said:

فَإِنِّي سَمِعْتُ دَفَّ نَعْلَيْكَ بَيْنَ يَدَيَّ فِي الْجَنَّةِ

I heard the scuffle of your sandals before me in Paradise.[13]

Thus Bilal ibn Rabah ﷺ enjoyed the close companionship of the Prophet ﷺ himself, played an important part in Islamic history during his life and was assured of his place in Jannah in the hereafter.

Receive the blessings, mercy and guidance of Allah ﷻ

These ayat highlight that when a person is patient through a trial they will receive the blessings, mercy, glad tidings and guidance of Allah ﷻ.

---

[13] The full hadith is: Abu Huraira ﷺ reported that the Prophet ﷺ said to Bilal at the time of dawn prayer, "O Bilal, tell me of the most hopeful deed you practiced in Islam. I heard the scuffle of your sandals before me in Paradise." Bilal said, "The most hopeful deed to me is that I do not perform ablution by day or night that I pray along with it as much as Allah decreed me to pray." (Sahih Bukhari)

وَلَنَبْلُوَنَّكُم بِشَيْءٍ مِّنَ ٱلْخَوْفِ وَٱلْجُوعِ وَنَقْصٍ مِّنَ ٱلْأَمْوَالِ وَٱلْأَنفُسِ وَٱلثَّمَرَاتِ ۗ وَبَشِّرِ ٱلصَّابِرِينَ ٱلَّذِينَ إِذَآ أَصَابَتْهُم مُّصِيبَةٌ قَالُوٓا۟ إِنَّا لِلَّهِ وَإِنَّآ إِلَيْهِ رَاجِعُونَ أُو۟لَٰٓئِكَ عَلَيْهِمْ صَلَوَٰتٌ مِّن رَّبِّهِمْ وَرَحْمَةٌ ۖ وَأُو۟لَٰٓئِكَ هُمُ ٱلْمُهْتَدُونَ

We will test you with a certain amount of fear and hunger and loss of wealth and life and fruits. But give good news to the steadfast: Those who, when disaster strikes them, say, "We belong to Allah and to Him we will return." Those are the people who will have blessings and mercy from their Lord; they are the ones who are guided.

(Surah al-Baqarah 2:155-157)

About this, one of the salaf said: *"Why should I not practice patience, when Allah has promised those who have patience three rewards, each of which is better than this world and everything in it? Blessings, Mercy and Guidance.*[14]

These are some of the vast benefits that come from being afflicted with trials and patiently working through them. The fruits of patiently bearing hardship are not only reaped in the hereafter, but can be felt and enjoyed in this world as well.

---

14 Ibn Qayyim Al-Jawziyyah, trans. Nasiruddin Al-Khattab, *Patience and Gratitude* (Ta-Ha Publishers Ltd, London, 1997) p.40

The Path of the Blessed

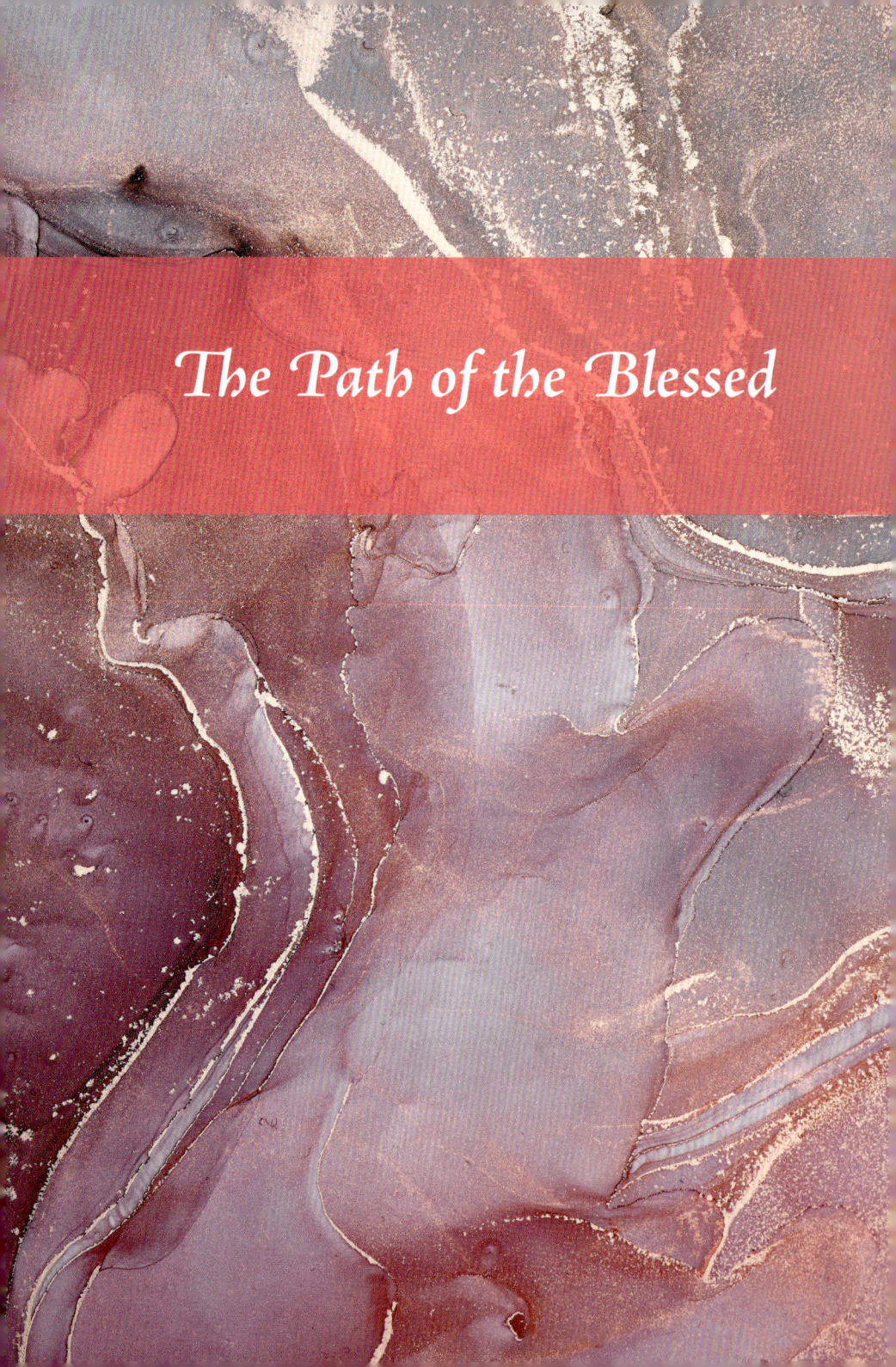

$$\text{أَحَسِبَ ٱلنَّاسُ أَن يُتْرَكُوٓا۟ أَن يَقُولُوٓا۟ ءَامَنَّا وَهُمْ لَا يُفْتَنُونَ وَلَقَدْ فَتَنَّا ٱلَّذِينَ مِن قَبْلِهِمْ فَلَيَعْلَمَنَّ ٱللَّهُ ٱلَّذِينَ صَدَقُوا۟ وَلَيَعْلَمَنَّ ٱلْكَٰذِبِينَ}$$

Do people imagine that they will be left to say, "We believe", and will not be tested? We tested those before them so that Allah would know the truthful and would know the liars.
(Surah al-Ankabut 29:2-3)

From this ayah, it is clear that it is not enough to profess belief. The strength of a person's iman can only be known when it is put to the test and it is these tests that separate those who simply say they believe from those who truly have iman in their hearts.

Islamic history gives us a glimpse into the levels of hardship that were endured by the early Muslims who were subjected to immense torture as a result of their beliefs. One such story is that of Khabbab ibn al-Arat ﷺ. Khabbab ﷺ would have his back burnt with hot iron rods as a torture method to try to get him to forsake Islam. This sahabah, who had to undergo so much hardship, went to the Prophet ﷺ for help. In order to provide solace, the Prophet reminded him of the righteous people of the past who had to undergo immense trials and through the strength of their iman became successful in this life and the next.

قَالَ شَكَوْنَا إِلَى رَسُولِ اللهِ ﷺ وَهْوَ مُتَوَسِّدٌ بُرْدَةً لَهُ فِي ظِلِّ الْكَعْبَةِ قُلْنَا لَهُ أَلاَ تَسْتَنْصِرُ لَنَا أَلاَ تَدْعُو اللهَ لَنَا قَالَ كَانَ الرَّجُلُ فِيمَنْ قَبْلَكُمْ يُحْفَرُ لَهُ فِي الأَرْضِ فَيُجْعَلُ فِيهِ فَيُجَاءُ بِالْمِنْشَارِ فَيُوضَعُ عَلَى رَأْسِهِ فَيُشَقُّ بِاثْنَتَيْنِ وَمَا يَصُدُّهُ ذَلِكَ عَنْ دِينِهِ وَيُمْشَطُ بِأَمْشَاطِ الْحَدِيدِ مَا دُونَ لَحْمِهِ مِنْ عَظْمٍ أَوْ عَصَبٍ وَمَا يَصُدُّهُ ذَلِكَ عَنْ دِينِهِ وَاللهِ لَيُتِمَّنَّ هَذَا الأَمْرَ حَتَّى يَسِيرَ الرَّاكِبُ مِنْ صَنْعَاءَ إِلَى حَضْرَمَوْتَ لاَ يَخَافُ إِلاَّ اللهَ أَوِ الذِّئْبَ عَلَى غَنَمِهِ وَلَكِنَّكُمْ تَسْتَعْجِلُونَ

Narrated Khabbab bin al-Arat:

We complained to Allah's Messenger ﷺ (of the persecution inflicted on us by the infidels) while he was sitting in the shade of the Ka'bah, leaning over his Burd (i.e. covering sheet). We said to him, "Would you seek help for us? Would you pray to Allah for us?" He said, "Among the nations before you a (believing) man would be put in a ditch that was dug for him, and a saw would be put over his head and he would be cut into two pieces; yet that (torture) would not make him give up his religion. His body would be combed with iron combs that would remove his flesh from the bones and nerves, yet that would not make him abandon his religion. By Allah, this religion (i.e. Islam) will prevail till a traveller from Sana (in Yemen) to Hadramaut will fear none but Allah, or a wolf as regards his sheep, but you (people) are hasty."

(Sahih Bukhari)

Allah describes the level of trials and difficulties that the righteous of the past have suffered:

أَمْ حَسِبْتُمْ أَن تَدْخُلُوا۟ ٱلْجَنَّةَ وَلَمَّا يَأْتِكُم مَّثَلُ ٱلَّذِينَ خَلَوْا۟ مِن قَبْلِكُم ۖ مَّسَّتْهُمُ ٱلْبَأْسَآءُ وَٱلضَّرَّآءُ وَزُلْزِلُوا۟ حَتَّىٰ يَقُولَ ٱلرَّسُولُ وَٱلَّذِينَ ءَامَنُوا۟ مَعَهُۥ مَتَىٰ نَصْرُ ٱللَّهِ ۗ أَلَآ إِنَّ نَصْرَ ٱللَّهِ قَرِيبٌ

Or did you suppose that you would enter the Garden without facing the same as those who came before you? Poverty and illness afflicted them and they were shaken to the point that the Messenger and those who believed with him said, "When is Allah's help coming?" Be assured that Allah's help is very near.
(Surah al-Baqarah 2:214)

The Qur'an describes so vividly the level of trials the righteous of the past had to undergo. It is mentioned they were زُلْزِلُوا۟ – shaken – which is the same word used for an earthquake. Imagine the intensity with which their very souls were shaken and yet Allah's ﷻ help came to them. This is the reassurance and solace we need to seek when we are similarly shaken to the core from a trial – that Allah's ﷻ help is near.

The closer we are to Allah ﷻ, the greater tests we will face in this life:

يَا رَسُولَ اللَّهِ أَيُّ النَّاسِ أَشَدُّ بَلَاءً قَالَ رَسُولُ اللَّهِ ﷺ الْأَنْبِيَاءُ ثُمَّ الْأَمْثَلُ فَالْأَمْثَلُ فَيُبْتَلَى الرَّجُلُ عَلَى حَسَبِ دِينِهِ فَإِنْ كَانَ دِينُهُ صُلْبًا اشْتَدَّ بَلَاؤُهُ وَإِنْ كَانَ فِي دِينِهِ رِقَّةٌ ابْتُلِيَ عَلَى حَسَبِ دِينِهِ فَمَا يَبْرَحُ الْبَلَاءُ بِالْعَبْدِ حَتَّى يَتْرُكَهُ يَمْشِي عَلَى الْأَرْضِ مَا عَلَيْهِ خَطِيئَةٌ

Sa'id ibn Abi Waqqas ﷺ reported: I said, "O Messenger of Allah, which people are tested most severely?" The Messenger of Allah ﷺ said, "They are the prophets, then the next best, then the next best. A man is put to trial according to his religion. If he is firm in his religion, his trials will be more severe. If he is weak in his religion, he is put to trial according to his strength in religion. The servant will continue to be put to trial until he is left walking upon the earth without any sin."
(Sunan at-Tirmidhi)

Going into detail into the lives of the righteous and the tests they had to undergo is beyond the scope of this small work so the reader is encouraged to read up on the lives of the prophets and the righteous. However, it is worth taking a brief look at a few examples of how some of the best people on earth responded in the face of their trials.

Prophet Ayyub's ﷺ sickness

Ayyub ﷺ, the beloved Prophet of Allah ﷻ, suffered loss in his health, wealth, family and place in society. He ﷺ was afflicted with a disease that caused him to lose almost everything he had. In his time of affliction and pain, he called to Allah ﷻ for help and the Qur'an captures the words of his du'a.

وَأَيُّوبَ إِذْ نَادَىٰ رَبَّهُۥٓ أَنِّى مَسَّنِىَ ٱلضُّرُّ وَأَنتَ أَرْحَمُ ٱلرَّٰحِمِينَ

And Ayyub when he called out to his Lord, "Great harm has afflicted me, but You are the Most Merciful of the merciful."

(Surah al-Anbiya 21:83)

What is significant is that in his period of suffering, Ayyub ﷺ acknowledges that Allah ﷻ is the Most Merciful of those who show mercy. Through his patience, Allah ﷻ restored his health, wealthy, family to him in an even a better state than before.

Maryam's (alayhas salaam) pain

When Maryam (alayhas salaam) was pregnant with Isa ﷺ, she had to suffer the pangs of childbirth by herself, which must have been an extremely difficult experience to undergo as a young woman. Along with the physical pain of childbirth, Maryam (alayhas salaam) also had to deal with her anxiety in facing her community and the accusations that would follow the miraculous birth of Isa ﷺ. In those moments of intense physical pain and psychological pressure with no human being to support her, she uttered words that will be forever preserved in the Book of Allah ﷻ.

فَأَجَاءَهَا ٱلْمَخَاضُ إِلَىٰ جِذْعِ ٱلنَّخْلَةِ قَالَتْ يَٰلَيْتَنِي مِتُّ قَبْلَ هَٰذَا وَكُنتُ نَسْيًا مَّنسِيًّا

The pains of labour drove her to the trunk of a date palm. She said, "Oh if only I had died before this time and were something discarded and forgotten!"
(Surah Maryam 19:23)

Imagine how lonely and unsupported she must have felt to have said such words. Yet this period of great trial led to the birth of the Isa ﷺ, who is revered by half the world. Maryam (alayhas salaam), who had to live with the fear of being castigated by her own community, was rewarded with paradise.

$$\text{أَفْضَلُ نِسَاءِ أَهْلِ الْجَنَّةِ خَدِيجَةُ بِنْتُ خُوَيْلِدٍ وَفَاطِمَةُ بِنْتُ مُحَمَّدٍ وَمَرْيَمُ بِنْتُ عِمْرَانَ وَآسِيَةُ بِنْتُ مُزَاحِمٍ امْرَأَةُ فِرْعَوْنَ}$$

Ibn Abbas ؓ reported that the Messenger of Allah ﷺ said:
The best of women among the people of Paradise are Khadijah bint Khuwaylid, Fatimah bint Muhammad, Maryam bint 'Imran, and 'Asiyah bint Muzahim, the wife of Pharaoh.
(Musnad Ahmad)

In fact all the women mentioned in the hadith suffered enormous trials in their different ways but faced them with grace and fortitude.

Prophet Yaqub's ؑ separation

We have all experienced the pain and sadness that accompanies separation from a loved one. Imagine this pain manifest at a far greater level by the Prophet Yaqub ؑ when he was separated from his beloved son, Prophet Yusuf ؑ, knowing he was alive but not in what condition or state. Prophet Yaqub's ؑ sadness and tears reached such a level that he became blind. In this desperate state, he said the following:

$$\text{قَالَ إِنَّمَآ أَشْكُوا بَثِّي وَحُزْنِي إِلَى ٱللَّهِ وَأَعْلَمُ مِنَ ٱللَّهِ مَا لَا تَعْلَمُونَ}$$

He said, "I make complaint about my grief and sorrow to Allah alone because I know things from Allah that you do not know."

(Surah Yusuf 12:83)

This is an important point to note that it is a part of the human condition to feel grief and pain in times of hardship. Even the prophets felt this way. However, Prophet Yaqub ﷺ complained only to Allah ﷻ, the only One that can change our situation and the only One that fully understands our pain. Complaining to Allah ﷻ does not contradict patience or show ingratitude. Rather complaining to Allah ﷻ in difficult times shows our deep connection with our Creator, trusting and turning to Him alone in the Knowledge that He alone can help. It is a manifestation of what we utter several times a day in Surah al-Fatihah:

$$\text{إِيَّاكَ نَعْبُدُ وَإِيَّاكَ نَسْتَعِينُ}$$

You alone we worship and You alone we ask for help.

(Surah al-Fatihah 1:4)

Eventually Yaqub ﷺ was reunited with his beloved son, Yusuf ﷺ. Now arguably this meeting could have happened at any time during Yusuf's ﷺ life. However, Allah ﷻ chose to reunite him with his father after his imprisonment was over and he had achieved a high position in the kingdom of Egypt. Thus Yaqub ﷺ was able to witness his son flourish and achieve great heights both spiritually and materially.

The best of creation ﷺ

The Prophet Muhammad ﷺ is the best of creation, a mercy to all the worlds, the beloved of Allah ﷻ, the leader of mankind and the Seal of the Prophets. Yet despite having such a high status, he ﷺ experienced the most suffering and grieved the most for the guidance of mankind.

He ﷺ was born an orphan and experienced the loss of those most dear to him throughout his life; from his mother at the age of six, his grandfather, his uncle, his infant sons, two of his beloved wives and three of his four daughters. He ﷺ witnessed his close companions be tortured and killed for their faith; he ﷺ was persecuted by his own relatives and community and to those he ﷺ preached to the point that his sandals were filled with blood; he ﷺ suffered hunger and made do with little. Yet he ﷺ always worried for his people. The Qur'an states his grief for the guidance for humanity was so intense that it would kill him.

فَلَعَلَّكَ بَٰخِعٌ نَّفْسَكَ عَلَىٰٓ ءَاثَٰرِهِمْ إِن لَّمْ يُؤْمِنُوا۟ بِهَٰذَا ٱلْحَدِيثِ أَسَفًا

Perhaps you may destroy yourself with grief, chasing after them, if they do not believe in these words.
(Surah al-Kahf 18:6)

However, the response of the Prophet ﷺ in the face of grief was gratitude as this hadith about the passing of his beloved son, Ibrahim, shows:

دَخَلْنَا مَعَ رَسُولِ اللَّهِ ﷺ عَلَى أَبِي سَيْفِ الْقَيْنِ وَكَانَ ظِئْرًا لِإِبْرَاهِيمَ عَلَيْهِ السَّلَامُ فَأَخَذَ رَسُولُ اللَّهِ ﷺ إِبْرَاهِيمَ فَقَبَّلَهُ وَشَمَّهُ ثُمَّ دَخَلْنَا عَلَيْهِ بَعْدَ ذَلِكَ وَإِبْرَاهِيمُ يَجُودُ بِنَفْسِهِ فَجَعَلَتْ عَيْنَا رَسُولِ اللَّهِ ﷺ تَذْرِفَانِ فَقَالَ لَهُ عَبْدُ الرَّحْمَنِ بْنُ عَوْفٍ ﷺ عَنْهُ وَأَنْتَ يَا رَسُولَ اللَّهِ فَقَالَ يَا ابْنَ عَوْفٍ إِنَّهَا رَحْمَةٌ ثُمَّ أَتْبَعَهَا بِأُخْرَى فَقَالَ ﷺ إِنَّ الْعَيْنَ تَدْمَعُ وَالْقَلْبَ يَحْزَنُ وَلَا نَقُولُ إِلَّا مَا يَرْضَى رَبُّنَا وَإِنَّا بِفِرَاقِكَ يَا إِبْرَاهِيمُ لَمَحْزُونُونَ

Anas ibn Malik ﷺ reported:
We entered the house of Abu Sayf, along with the Messenger of Allah ﷺ, who was the husband of Ibrahim's wet-nurse, upon him be peace. The Prophet took hold of Ibrahim, kissed him, and smelled him. Then, we entered after that as Ibrahim was breathing his last breaths. It made the eyes of the Prophet shed tears. 'Abdur Rahman ibn 'Awf said, "Even you, O Messenger of Allah?" The Prophet said, "O Ibn 'Awf, this is mercy." Then, the Prophet wept some more and he said, "Verily, the eyes shed tears and the heart is grieved, but we will not say anything except what is pleasing to our Lord. We are saddened by your departure, O Ibrahim."
(Sahih Bukhari)

For any believer who wishes to find solace in their darkest hour, reading an account of the life of the Prophet of Allah ﷺ will show us that the beloved of Allah ﷺ went through far greater trials than any of us can ever experience. His ﷺ immense suffering did not deter him from establishing the truth and reforming an ignorant society, while being the model father, husband and leader.

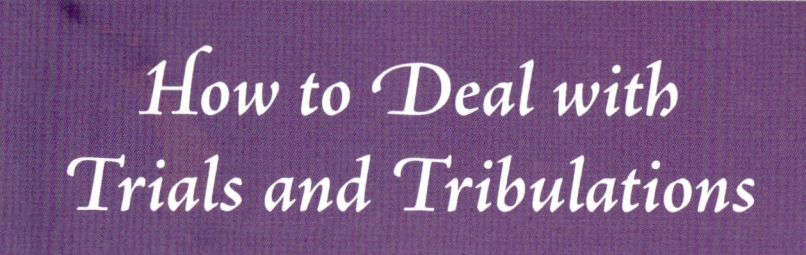

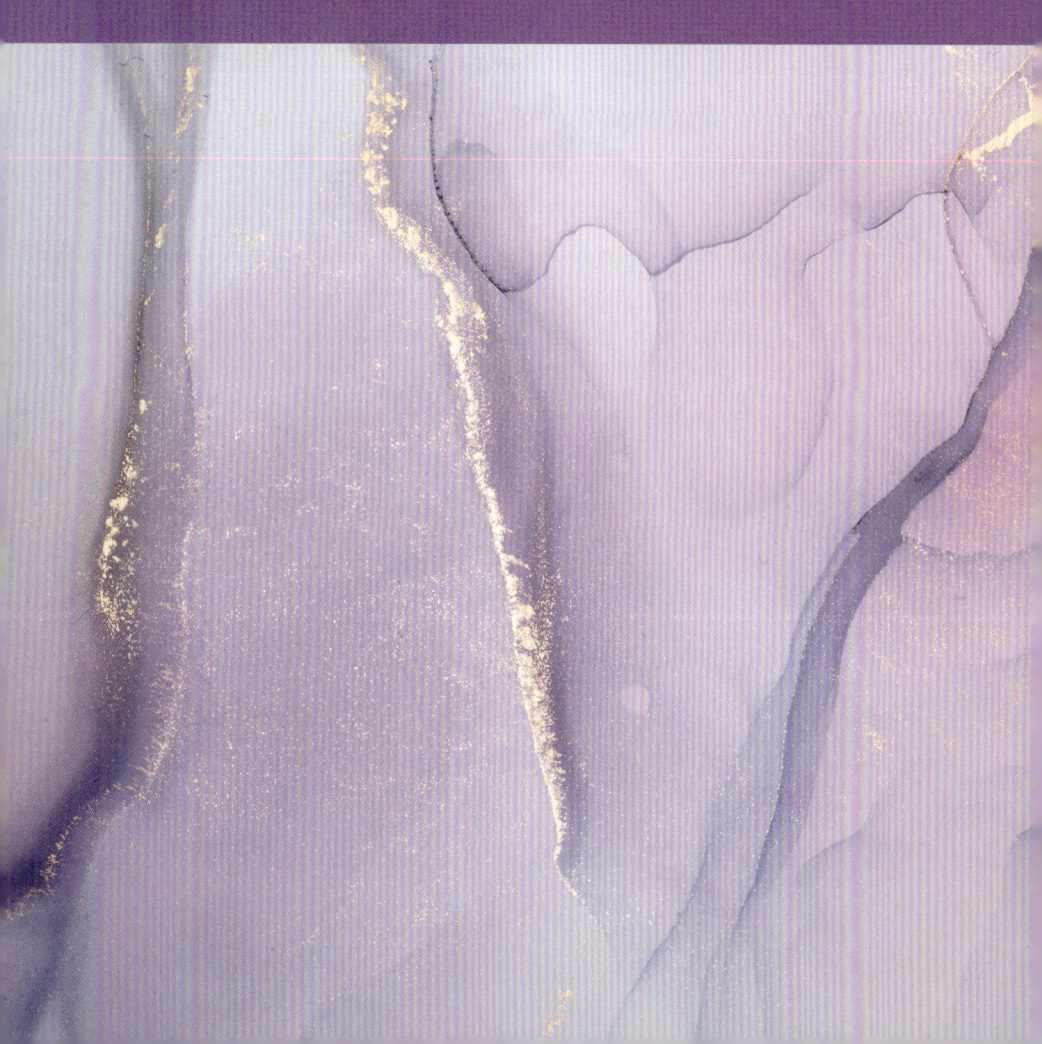

How to Deal with Trials and Tribulations

Having gained a thorough understanding of why trials afflict us and how the most righteous people have overcome their difficult periods, we will now look at some practical methods on how to deal with trials and tribulations as shown to us from the Qur'an and Sunnah.

Du'a

وَقَالَ رَبُّكُمُ ادْعُونِي أَسْتَجِبْ لَكُمْ إِنَّ الَّذِينَ يَسْتَكْبِرُونَ عَنْ عِبَادَتِي سَيَدْخُلُونَ جَهَنَّمَ دَاخِرِينَ

Your Lord says, "Call on Me and I will answer you. Those who are too proud to worship Me will enter Hell abject."
(Surah Ghafir 40:60)

The first and foremost thing to do in times of difficulty is to call on Allah ﷻ. He ﷻ has promised to respond. When we ask a fellow human being to help, they may respond once or twice, but if we keep repeatedly asking them for help, they will avoid us. Allah ﷻ, on the other hand, wants us to ask and ask, and is displeased with us when we become too proud to ask.

When we ask, Allah ﷺ is ready to respond – he is not too occupied to attend his calling servant:

وَإِذَا سَأَلَكَ عِبَادِى عَنِّى فَإِنِّى قَرِيبٌ أُجِيبُ دَعْوَةَ ٱلدَّاعِ إِذَا دَعَانِ فَلْيَسْتَجِيبُوا لِى وَلْيُؤْمِنُوا بِى لَعَلَّهُمْ يَرْشُدُونَ

If my slaves ask you about me, I am near.
I answer the call of the caller when he calls
on Me. They should therefore respond
to me and believe in me so that hopefully
they will be rightly guided.
(Surah al-Baqarah 2:186)

In this ayah, Allah ﷻ starts by mentioning that He ﷻ responds to the call, before mentioning the act of calling Him ﷻ. In everyday language, we would construct a sentence in the order in which the actions took place – the act of calling followed by the act of responding. But here Allah ﷻ is showing His ﷻ willingness to answer our du'as. We just need to raise our hands to Him Who has said that He ﷻ is near. And exactly how near is He ﷻ?

وَلَقَدْ خَلَقْنَا ٱلْإِنسَٰنَ وَنَعْلَمُ مَا تُوَسْوِسُ بِهِۦ نَفْسُهُۥ ۖ وَنَحْنُ أَقْرَبُ إِلَيْهِ مِنْ حَبْلِ ٱلْوَرِيدِ

We created man and We know what his own self whispers to him. We are nearer to him than his jugular vein.
(Surah Qaf 50:16)

The jugular vein is that vital vein in the body which pumps blood to the heart and which, if it is severed, results in our immediate death. Our connection to Allah ﷻ is more vital than even our jugular vein and if we try to sever our relationship with Allah ﷻ, we end up killing ourselves spiritually.[15]

---

15 Y. Mogahed, *Reclaim your Heart* (FB Publishing, San Clemente, 2015) p.102

We have discussed that Allah is Al-Kareem, The Most Generous, and He ﷻ wants to give and the fact that He ﷻ has inspired you to call upon Him ﷻ means that He ﷻ is just waiting to give. Ibn Ata'illah states regarding du'a: *If He allows you to ask, then know that He wants to give you something.*¹⁶

Salman al-Farsi ؓ reported the Messenger of Allah ﷺ as saying:

إِنَّ اللَّهَ حَيِيٌّ كَرِيمٌ يَسْتَحْيِي إِذَا رَفَعَ الرَّجُلُ إِلَيْهِ يَدَيْهِ أَنْ يَرُدَّهُمَا صِفْرًا خَائِبَتَيْنِ

Verily, Allah is Munificent and Generous. He would be ashamed, when a man raises his hands to him, to turn them away empty and disappointed.
(Sunan at-Tirmidhi)

So from this, we can understand that Allah ﷻ will answer our call to Him ﷻ. However, this is different from Him ﷻ giving us what we ask for. If we simply made du'a and Allah ﷻ answered it, then there is no mercy in that and that is to misunderstand His Majesty. We may ask for something that is not good for us; we may ask for something to satisfy our desires rather than something that will contribute to our spiritual growth; we may ask for what we want but we should understand that Allah ﷻ gives us what we need. That is because, as we have seen, He ﷻ is All-Knowing. So our du'as are answered in one of three ways as the following hadith explains:

---

16 J. Auda, *A Journey to God, Reflections on Hikam ibn Ata'illah* (Awakening Publications, UK, 2017) p.65

> مَا مِنْ مُسْلِمٍ يَدْعُو بِدَعْوَةٍ لَيْسَ فِيهَا إِثْمٌ وَلَا قَطِيعَةُ رَحِمٍ إِلَّا أَعْطَاهُ اللَّهُ بِهَا إِحْدَى ثَلَاثٍ إِمَّا أَنْ تُعَجَّلَ لَهُ دَعْوَتُهُ وَإِمَّا أَنْ يَدَّخِرَهَا لَهُ فِي الْآخِرَةِ وَإِمَّا أَنْ يَصْرِفَ عَنْهُ مِنَ السُّوءِ مِثْلَهَا قَالُوا إِذًا نُكْثِرُ قَالَ اللَّهُ أَكْثَرُ

Abu Sa'id al-Khudri ؓ reported
the Messenger of Allah ﷺ said:
*There is no Muslim who calls upon Allah,
without sin or cutting family ties, but that Allah
will give him one of three answers:
He will quickly fulfil his supplication,
He will store it for him in the Hereafter,
or He will divert an evil from him similar to it.*
They said, "In that case we will ask for more."
The Prophet said, "Allah has even more."
(Musnad Ahmad)

The very act of making du'a is a blessing in itself because it is a means through which you can communicate directly with your Lord, open your heart to Him ﷻ, seek solace in Him ﷻ, be vulnerable and know that He ﷻ is listening and responding and your pleas are safe with Him ﷻ. There is no human on earth with whom we can be guaranteed to have that relationship with throughout our lives.

As human beings, we tend to call on Allah ﷻ with greater intensity in our moments of weakness and helplessness. Allah ﷻ assures us of His ﷻ response at these moments of despair:

أَمَّن يُجِيبُ ٱلْمُضْطَرَّ إِذَا دَعَاهُ وَيَكْشِفُ ٱلسُّوٓءَ وَيَجْعَلُكُمْ خُلَفَآءَ ٱلْأَرْضِ أَءِلَٰهٌ مَّعَ ٱللَّهِ قَلِيلًا مَّا تَذَكَّرُونَ

He Who responds to the oppressed when they call on Him and removes their distress, and has appointed you as khalifs on the earth. Is there another god besides Allah? How little you pay heed!

(Surah an-Naml 27:62)

In a state of distress, we are more cognizant of our **'ubudiyyah** – our servitude and insignificance before Allah ﷻ – and when reach such a state our du'a will be filled with more sincerity. Although it is important to call on Allah ﷻ in our hour of difficulty, it is also important to note that we should be calling on Allah ﷻ in times of ease as well:

مَنْ سَرَّهُ أَنْ يَسْتَجِيبَ اللَّهُ لَهُ عِنْدَ الشَّدَائِدِ
وَالْكُرَبِ فَلْيُكْثِرِ الدُّعَاءَ فِي الرَّخَاءِ

Abu Huraira ؓ reported that the Messenger of Allah ﷺ said:
Whoever wishes that Allah respond to him during hardship and grief should supplicate plentifully when at ease.
(Sunan at-Tirmidhi)

It is disrespectful that we should call on Allah ﷻ in times of difficulty but then forget Him ﷻ in times of prosperity. As mentioned earlier, both difficulty and prosperity are tests to see whether we turn to Allah ﷻ or become heedless.

Prophetic Supplications

These are just a small selection of du'as that are prescribed in the Qur'an and hadith to help us when faced with trials and tribulations.

Du'a of Umm Salamah ؓ

Umm Salamah ؓ reported: I heard the Messenger of Allah ﷺ saying: "When a person suffers from a calamity and utters:

إِنَّا لِلَّهِ وَإِنَّا إِلَيْهِ رَاجِعُونَ اللَّهُمَّ أَجُرْنِي فِي مُصِيبَتِي وَأَخْلِفْ لِي خَيْرًا مِنْهَا

*Inna lillāh wa inna ilayhi rāji'un.
Allahumma ajurni fi muṣībati wa akhlif li khayran minha*

Indeed, to Allah we belong and to Allah we will return. (2:156)
O Allah, reward me in my affliction and replace it with something better than it.

Then Allah will surely replace it for him with that which is better."

Umm Salamah ؓ said: When Abu Salamah ؓ died, I repeated the same supplication as the Messenger of Allah ﷺ had commanded me (to do), so Allah bestowed upon me a better substitute than him. (Sahih Muslim)

This du'a was taught to Umm Salamah ؓ by the Prophet ﷺ when she lost her husband Abu Salamah ؓ, who passed away from a wound he received in the Battle of Uhud. She loved Abu Salamah ؓ greatly and could not imagine the thought of anyone ever being able to replace him. Later, she was blessed to marry the best of creation, the Prophet ﷺ and became Umm al-Mu'mineen – a mother of the believers.

Du'a of Prophet Yunus عليه السلام

Sa'd ؓ reported that the Messenger of Allah ﷺ said: "The supplication of Yunus عليه السلام when he called upon Allah inside the belly of the whale was this:

$$\text{لَّا إِلَٰهَ إِلَّا أَنتَ سُبْحَٰنَكَ إِنِّى كُنتُ مِنَ ٱلظَّٰلِمِينَ}$$

La ilāha illa anta subḥanaka innī kuntu minaẓ-ẓalimeen

**There is no god but You! Glory be to You!
Truly I have been one of the wrongdoers.**
(Surah al-Anbiya 21:87)

Verily, a Muslim never supplicates for anything with it but that Allah will answer him." (Sunan at-Tirmidhi)

This du'a of Yunus عليه السلام is very powerful and was uttered when he was covered in three layers of darkness – the depth of darkness of the night, the darkness of the ocean and the darkness of the belly of the whale. Yunus عليه السلام called on Allah ﷻ through this du'a and Allah ﷻ saved him and brought him out of the belly of the whale with the following reassurance to all believers who recite this du'a:

$$\text{فَٱسْتَجَبْنَا لَهُۥ وَنَجَّيْنَٰهُ مِنَ ٱلْغَمِّ وَكَذَٰلِكَ نُـۨجِى ٱلْمُؤْمِنِينَ}$$

**We responded to him and rescued him from his grief.
That is how We rescue the believers.**
(Surah al-Anbiya 21:88)

Entrusting your affairs to Allah ﷻ

Abu Bakrah ؓ reported that the Messenger of Allah ﷺ said: "The supplications of the one in distress are:

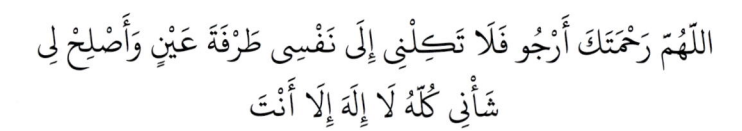

اللَّهُمَّ رَحْمَتَكَ أَرْجُو فَلَا تَكِلْنِي إِلَى نَفْسِي طَرْفَةَ عَيْنٍ وَأَصْلِحْ لِي شَأْنِي كُلَّهُ لَا إِلَهَ إِلَا أَنْتَ

Allahumma raḥmataka arjū falā takilnī ilā nafsī tarfata 'aynin wa aṣliḥ lī sha'ni kullahu lā ilāha ilā anta

O Allah, it is Your mercy that I hope for, so do not leave me in charge of my affairs even for a blink of an eye and rectify for me all of my affairs. None has the right to be worshipped except You." (Ibn Hibban)

In this du'a, we entrust Allah ﷻ with all our affairs and recognise that we cannot do anything by ourselves without His ﷻ help. Once we recognise that we are completely incapable of doing anything without the help of Allah, then we have understood the concept of **'ubudiyyah** – a state of servitude in which we are utterly weak and impoverished without the help of Allah ﷻ. Ibn Ata'illah said:

No matter is difficult if you seek it with through your Lord and no matter is easy if you seek it yourself.[17]

---

[17] Ibn 'Ataillah Al-Sakandari, *Al-Hikam Al-'Aatiyah* (Dar Al-Kotob Al-Ilmiyah, Beirut, 2002) p.50

Seeking refuge from anxiety and grief

Narrated Abu Sa'id al-Khudri ﷺ: One day the Messenger of Allah ﷺ entered the mosque. There he saw there a man from the Ansar called Abu Umamah. He said: "What is the matter that I am seeing you sitting in the mosque when there is no time of prayer?" He said: "I am entangled in worries and debts, Messenger of Allah." He ﷺ replied: "Shall I not teach you words by which, when you say them, Allah will remove your worries and settle your debt?" He said: "Why not, Messenger of Allah?" He ﷺ said: "Say in the morning and evening:

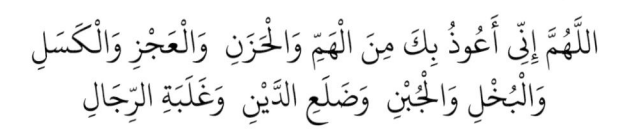

اللَّهُمَّ إِنِّي أَعُوذُ بِكَ مِنَ الْهَمِّ وَالْحَزَنِ وَالْعَجْزِ وَالْكَسَلِ وَالْبُخْلِ وَالْجُبْنِ وَضَلَعِ الدَّيْنِ وَغَلَبَةِ الرِّجَالِ

*Allahumma innī a'ūdhu bika minal hammi wal ḥazani,
wal 'ajzi wal kasali, wal bukhli wal jubni,
wa dhala'id-dayni wa ghalabatir-rijāl*

O Allah, I seek refuge in you from anxiety and grief, from weakness and from laziness, from miserliness and from cowardice, from being overcome by debt and overpowered by men (i.e. others)." (Sunan Abu Dawud)

This du'a of the Prophet ﷺ is comprehensive in that we are taught to seek refuge from several negative states, the first two being of interest with regards to the subject matter we are discussing. الْهَمّ – anxiety – is having negative expectations of future events while الْحَزَن – grief – is negative emotion relating to past events.[18] Most people who are incapacitated by negative emotions are usually regretful over the past or fearful for the future and so this du'a provides a means of remedy for both cases.

---
18 Al-Qarni, *La Tahzan* (Maktaba Al-Abeekan, 2003) p.73

Seeking refuge from sorrow and distress

Asma bint Umays ﷺ reported that the Prophet ﷺ asked her, "Shall I tell you words that you may say in times of sorrow (غُمٌّ) or distress (كَرْبٌ)? These are:

$$\text{اللهُ اللهُ رَبِّي لَا أُشْرِكُ بِهِ شَيْئًا}$$

Allāhu Allāhu rabbī, lā ushriku bihī shay'an

Allah, Allah is my Lord, I do not associate anything with Him."
(Sunan Abu Dawud)

Spring of the heart

'Abdullah ibn Mas'ud ﷺ reported that the Messenger of Allah ﷺ said: "No person suffers any anxiety or grief, and then says this du'a except that Allah will remove his sorrow and replace it with happiness:

$$\text{اَللّٰهُمَّ إِنِّيْ عَبْدُكَ وَابْنُ عَبْدِكَ وَ ابْنُ أَمَتِكَ نَاصِيَتِيْ بِيَدِكَ مَاضٍ فِيَّ حُكْمُكَ عَدْلٌ فِيَّ قَضَآؤُكَ اَسْأَلُكَ بِكُلِّ اسْمٍ هُوَلَكَ سَمَّيْتَ بِهِ نَفْسَكَ اَوْ اَنْزَلْتَهُ فِيْ كِتَابِكَ اَوْ عَلَّمْتَهُ اَحَدًا مِّنْ خَلْقِكَ اَوِ اسْتَأْثَرْتَ بِهِ فِيْ عِلْمِ الْغَيْبِ عِنْدَكَ اَنْ تَجْعَلَ الْقُرْآنَ الْعَظِيْمَ رَبِيْعَ قَلْبِيْ وَ نُوْرَ صَدْرِيْ وَ جَلَآءَ حُزْنِيْ وَ ذَهَابَ هَمِّيْ وَ غَمِّيْ}$$

Allahumma innī 'abduka wabnu 'abdika wabnu amatika naṣiyatī bi yadika māḍin fiyya ḥukmuka 'adlun fiyya qaḍā'uka as'aluka bi kulli ismin huwa laka sammayta bihi nafsaka aw anzaltahū fī kitabika aw 'allamtahū aḥadan min khalqika awis ta'tharta bihi fī 'ilmil-ghaybi 'indaka an taj'alal-Qur'anal-'aẓeema rabi'a qalbī wa nura ṣadrī wa jalā'a ḥuzni wa dhahaba hammī wa ghammī

O Allah, I am Your slave, son of Your male servant, and son of Your female servant. My forelock is in Your Hand. Your command for me prevails. Your judgement concerning me is just. I beseech You through every name You have, by which You have called Yourself, or which You have sent down in Your Book, or which You have taught to any one of Your creations, or which You have preferred to keep to Yourself among Your guarded secrets, to make the Great Qur'an the spring of my heart, the light of my chest, the remedy of my grief, and the dispeller of my anxiety and sorrow."

(At-Tabarani)

This du'a ends by giving us an insight as to how we can replace our sorrow with happiness and that is by connecting with the Qur'an. We are asking Allah ﷻ to make the Qur'an a means of lightening the burdens in our heart, of refreshing our tiredness and removing grief and sorrow. So this leads us to the next means of dealing with trials and tribulations.

Qur'an

The Qur'an is a cure for all ailments within our hearts, therefore it is vital that the Qur'an plays a central role in our lives, as we find in the Qur'an itself:

يَـٰٓأَيُّهَا ٱلنَّاسُ قَدْ جَآءَتْكُم مَّوْعِظَةٌ مِّن رَّبِّكُمْ وَشِفَآءٌ لِّمَا فِى ٱلصُّدُورِ وَهُدًى وَرَحْمَةٌ لِّلْمُؤْمِنِينَ

Mankind! Admonition has come to you from your Lord and also healing for you for what is in the breasts and guidance and mercy for the believers.

(Surah Yunus 10:57)

This means that we need to build an ongoing relationship with the Qur'an. The more we put into this relationship, the greater the benefits we will get out of it. It is the 'Spring of the Heart' – it will provide fresh hope, new growth, new life and beauty to our hearts – as if revived after a barren winter. Here are some suggestions as to how to incorporate the Qur'an into our daily lives.

1. First, we need to understand that the Qur'an is more than a book of rules or a collection of stories. What we hold in our hands is a miracle, unchanged in over 1400 years, the very Word of Allah ﷻ. It was revealed to guide us and teach us of the nature of our existence. Once we can absorb this immense concept, then only can we treat it with the reverence it deserves and know the power which it has:

لَوْ أَنزَلْنَا هَٰذَا ٱلْقُرْءَانَ عَلَىٰ جَبَلٍ لَّرَأَيْتَهُۥ خَٰشِعًا مُّتَصَدِّعًا مِّنْ خَشْيَةِ ٱللَّهِ

If we had sent down this Qur'an onto a mountain, you would have seen it humbled, crushed to pieces out of the fear of Allah.
(Surah al-Hashr 59:21)

2. Make time to recite the Qur'an in Arabic and to understand what it says. This may be more challenging for those who are less familiar with Arabic but it is important to persevere with this as A'ishah ؓ reported that the Prophet ﷺ said:

الْمَاهِرُ بِالْقُرْآنِ مَعَ السَّفَرَةِ الْكِرَامِ الْبَرَرَةِ وَالَّذِى يَقْرَؤُهُ يَتَتَعْتَعُ فِيهِ وَهُوَ عَلَيْهِ شَاقٌّ لَهُ أَجْرَانِ اثْنَانِ

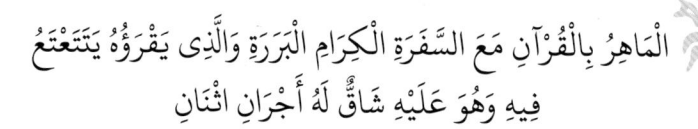

The one who is proficient with the Qur'an will be with the noble and righteous scribes (the angels), and the one who reads it and stumbles over it, finding it difficult, will have two rewards.
(Sunan Ibn Majah)

3. In those moments when we cannot sit and read the Qur'an, such as commuting to work or driving, then we can listen to the Qur'an (with translation, if needed). There are a wide variety of recitations that, not will not only help with the correct pronunciation, but will soothe the heart:

$$\text{وَإِذَا قُرِئَ ٱلْقُرْءَانُ فَٱسْتَمِعُوا۟ لَهُۥ وَأَنصِتُوا۟ لَعَلَّكُمْ تُرْحَمُونَ}$$

When the Qur'an is recited listen to it and be quiet so that hopefully you will gain mercy.
(Surah al-Araf 7:204)

4. We can gain an even deeper understanding of the Qur'an by reading a commentary of it; finding out the circumstances surrounding the revelation of certain ayat; understanding better what we have been commanded to do; drawing inspiration from the role models mentioned and pondering lessons taught:

$$\text{كِتَٰبٌ أَنزَلْنَٰهُ إِلَيْكَ مُبَٰرَكٌ لِّيَدَّبَّرُوٓا۟ ءَايَٰتِهِۦ وَلِيَتَذَكَّرَ أُو۟لُوا۟ ٱلْأَلْبَٰبِ}$$

It is a book we have sent down to you, full of blessing, so let people of intelligence ponder its Signs and take heed.
(Surah Sad 38:29)

Dhikr

We mentioned earlier that the heart by its nature is very unstable and the soul is restless. The only way to stabilise the heart and provide rest to the soul is through remembering Allah ﷻ for the heart's primary function is to know Allah ﷻ and the soul's source of agitations comes from being distant from Allah ﷻ.

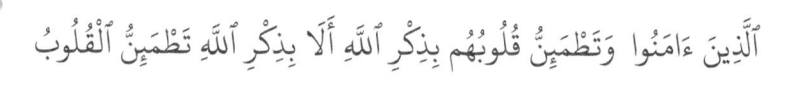

ٱلَّذِينَ ءَامَنُوا۟ وَتَطْمَئِنُّ قُلُوبُهُم بِذِكْرِ ٱللَّهِ أَلَا بِذِكْرِ ٱللَّهِ تَطْمَئِنُّ ٱلْقُلُوبُ

> Those who believe and whose hearts find peace in the remembrance of Allah. Only in the remembrance of Allah can the heart find peace.
> (Surah Ar-Ra'd 13:28)

Not only is dhikr a means of peace in this world, but it is also our key to paradise in the hereafter:

> Remembrance of Allah is His paradise on earth, and whoever does not enter it will not enter the Paradise of the Hereafter.[19]

In addition to reading the Qur'an and reciting the recommended du'as, we can engage our tongue with simple phrases while going about our daily business, either by simply reciting them, by counting them on our fingertips or on a tasbeeh (prayer beads). Counting these phrases on the fingers gives us the additional benefit of our fingers testifying on our behalf on the Day of Judgement, as Yusayrah bint Yasir ؓ reported that the Messenger of Allah ﷺ said:

---

[19] Al-Qarni, trans. Faisal ibn Muhammad Shafeeq, *Don't be Sad* (International Islamic Publishing House, Riyadh, 2005) p.122

$$\text{عَلَيْكُنَّ بِالتَّسْبِيحِ وَالتَّهْلِيلِ وَالتَّقْدِيسِ وَاعْقِدْنَ بِالْأَنَامِلِ فَإِنَّهُنَّ مَسْئُولَاتٌ مُسْتَنْطَقَاتٌ وَلَا تَغْفُلْنَ فَتَنْسَيْنَ الرَّحْمَةَ}$$

You must glorify Allah and declare the oneness and holiness of Allah. Count them on your fingers. Verily, the fingers will be questioned and made to speak. Do not be neglectful, such that you forget the mercy of Allah.
(Sunan at-Tirmidhi)

***

Abu Huraira reported that Allah's Messenger said, "Whoever says

$$\text{سُبْحَانَ ٱللَّهِ وَبِحَمْدِهِ}$$

Subḥānallāhi wa biḥamdihī
Glory be to Allah and praise Him

one hundred times a day, will be forgiven all his sins even if they were as much as the foam of the sea." (Sahih Bukhari)

***

It was narrated that Anas bin Malik said: "*Umm Sulaim came to the Prophet and said, "O Messenger of Allah, teach me some words that I may supplicate with during my prayer." He said, "Glorify Allah (by saying SubhanAllah) ten times, and praise Him (by saying Alhamdulillah) ten times, and magnify Him (by saying Allahu Akbar) ten times, then ask Him for what you need. He will say: 'Yes, yes.'"* (Sunan an-Nasa'i)

$$\text{سُبْحَانَ ٱللَّهِ ٱلْحَمْدُ لِلَّهِ ٱللَّهُ أَكْبَرُ}$$

Subḥānallah, Alḥamdulillāh, Allāhu Akbar
Glory be to Allah, Praise be to Allah, Allah is the Greatest

***

Abu Huraira ﷺ reported that the Messenger of Allah ﷺ said: "When a person sincerely says

لَا إِلَٰهَ إِلَّا ٱللَّهُ

Lā ilāha illallāh

There is no god but Allah

the doors of the sky are opened for it until it reaches the Throne so long as he avoids major sins." (Sunan at-Tirmidhī)

***

Abu Huraira ﷺ reported that the Messenger of Allah ﷺ said: "Increase in saying

$$\text{لَا حَوْلَ وَلَا قُوَّةَ إِلَّا بِٱللَّهِ ٱلْعَلِيِّ ٱلْعَظِيمِ}$$

Lā ḥawla wa lā quwwata illā billāh

There is no power nor strength except by Allah

for it is a treasure from the treasures of Paradise." (Musnad Ahmad)

***

Ibn 'Abbas ﷺ narrated that: When Ibrahim ﷺ was thrown into the fire, he ﷺ said

$$\text{حَسْبُنَا ٱللَّهُ وَنِعْمَ ٱلْوَكِيلُ}$$

Ḥasbunallāhu wa ni'mal wakeel

Allah (Alone) is sufficient for us and He is the Best Disposer of affairs

So did the Messenger of Allah when he was told: "A great army of the pagans had gathered against him, so fear them". But this (warning) only increased him and the Muslims in Faith and they said

$$\text{حَسْبُنَا ٱللَّهُ وَنِعْمَ ٱلْوَكِيلُ}$$

Ḥasbunallāhu wa ni'mal wakeel

Allah (Alone) is sufficient for us and He is the Best Disposer of affairs.
(Sahih Bukhari)

***

$$\text{وَلِلَّهِ ٱلْأَسْمَآءُ ٱلْحُسْنَىٰ فَٱدْعُوهُ بِهَا}$$

To Allah belong the Most Beautiful Names so call on Him by them.
(Surah al-Araf 7:180)

We can call on Allah ﷻ using any or all of His Beautiful Names and the Prophet ﷺ recommended the following:

Anas bin Malik ؓ said: "Whenever a matter would distress him, the Prophet ﷺ would say

$$\text{يَا حَيُّ يَا قَيُّومُ بِرَحْمَتِكَ أَسْتَغِيثُ}$$

Yā Ḥayyu, Yā Qayyūmu biraḥmatika astageeth

O Living, O Self-Sustaining Sustainer! In Your Mercy do I seek relief

Then he said: "The Messenger of Allah ﷺ said: 'Be constant with

$$\text{يَا ذَا الْجَلَالِ وَالْإِكْرَامِ}$$

Yā Dhal Jalāli wal Ikrām

O Possessor of Majesty and Honour.'"
(Sunan at-Tirmidhi)

Istighfar

The Prophet ﷺ prescribed istighfar (seeking forgiveness) as a means of removing anxiety and to be saved from hardship:

مَنْ أَكْثَرَ مِنَ الِاسْتِغْفَارِ جَعَلَ اللَّهُ لَهُ مِنْ كُلِّ هَمٍّ فَرَجًا وَمِنْ كُلِّ ضِيقٍ مَخْرَجًا وَرَزَقَهُ مِنْ حَيْثُ لَا يَحْتَسِبُ

Ibn Abbas ؓ reported that the Messenger of Allah ﷺ said: *Whoever increases his prayers for forgiveness, Allah will grant him relief from every worry, a way out from every hardship, and provide for him in ways he does not expect.* (Musnad Ahmad)

The power of istighfar is that, if done sincerely, it can remove all our sins no matter how great or numerous.

يَا ابْنَ آدَمَ إِنَّكَ مَا دَعَوْتَنِي وَرَجَوْتَنِي غَفَرْتُ لَكَ عَلَى مَا كَانَ مِنْكَ وَلَا أُبَالِي يَا ابْنَ آدَمَ لَوْ بَلَغَتْ ذُنُوبُكَ عَنَانَ السَّمَاءِ ثُمَّ اسْتَغْفَرْتَنِي غَفَرْتُ لَكَ يَا ابْنَ آدَمَ إِنَّكَ لَوْ أَتَيْتَنِي بِقُرَابِ الْأَرْضِ خَطَايَا ثُمَّ لَقِيتَنِي لَا تُشْرِكُ بِي شَيْئًا لَأَتَيْتُكَ بِقُرَابِهَا مَغْفِرَةً

Anas ibn Malik ؓ reported that the Messenger of Allah ﷺ said: *Allah the Almighty said: O son of Adam, so long as you call upon Me and ask of Me, I shall forgive you for what you have done, and I shall not mind. O son of Adam, were your sins to reach the clouds of the sky and were you then to ask forgiveness of Me, I would forgive you. O son of Adam, were you to come to Me with sins nearly as great as the earth and were you then to face Me, ascribing no partner to Me, I would bring you forgiveness nearly as great as it.* (Sunan at-Tirmidhi)

The word ghafara – غَفَرَ – means 'to cover, shield or protect'.[20] By seeking istighfar, we are actually seeking to be protected from our wrong actions and their consequences; for our faults to be covered from others; for our dignity to be shielded. Furthermore, it is a means through which we can rise up when we have sunk through our sins, as Ibn al-Qayyim has said:

Satan rejoiced when Adam ﷺ came out of Paradise, but he did not know that when a diver sinks into the sea, he collects pearls and then rises again.[21]

There are several phrases that can be used, the easiest and shortest of which are as follows.

In a hadith narrated by Thawban ﷺ, Imam al-Auza'i asked: "How should forgiveness be sought?" He replied, "I say:

أَسْتَغْفِرُ اللَّه ، أَسْتَغْفِرُ اللَّه

Astaghfirullāh, Astaghfirullāh

I seek forgiveness from Allah."
(Sahih Muslim)

***

---

[20] E. W. Lane, *An Arabic-English Lexicon* (Librairie du Liban, Beirut, 1968) Vol. 6, p.2273 and Imam Al-Raghib Al-Isfahani, *Mufradat Alfaz ul-Quran* (Dar Al-Qalam, Damascus, 2009) p.609
[21] Y. Mogahed, *Reclaim your Heart* (FB Publishing, San Clemente, 2015) p.64

A'ishah reported: "Prior to his demise, the Messenger of Allah used to supplicate frequently

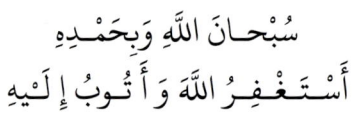

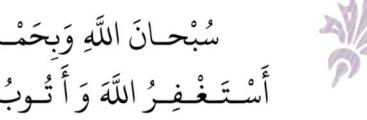

سُبْحَانَ اللَّهِ وَبِحَمْدِهِ
أَسْتَغْفِرُ اللَّهَ وَأَتُوبُ إِلَيْهِ

Subḥānallāhi wa biḥamdihī
Astaghfirullāha wa atūbu ilayhi

Glory be to Allah and praise Him
I seek forgiveness from Allah and I turn to him in repentance."
(Sahih Bukhari and Muslim)

***

Ibn 'Umar said: "We counted the Messenger saying a hundred times during one single sitting

رَبِّ اغْفِرْ لِي وَتُبْ عَلَيَّ إِنَّكَ أَنْتَ التَّوَّابُ الرَّحِيمُ

Rabbighfirlī wa tubb 'alayya innaka antat tawwābur raḥeem

My Lord! Forgive me and pardon me. Indeed, You are the Oft-Returning with compassion and Ever Merciful."
(Sunan Abu Dawud and at-Tirmidhi)

Salawat

مَنْ صَلَّى عَلَيَّ وَاحِدَةً صَلَّى اللَّهُ عَلَيْهِ عَشْرًا

'Abdullah bin 'Amr ibn al-'As ﷺ reported:
I heard the Messenger of Allah saying:
Whoever supplicates Allah to exalt my mention,
Allah will exalt his mention ten times.
(Sahih Muslim)

The virtue of sending blessings on the Prophet ﷺ is that Allah ﷻ Himself will send blessings on them. How can a person ever be miserable if Allah ﷻ is blessing them?

One of the recommended wordings for sending salawat on the Prophet ﷺ is:

Narrated 'Abdur-Rahman ibn Abi Laila: Ka'b bin Ujrah met me and said, "Shall I not give you a present I got from the Prophet?" 'Abdur-Rahman said, "Yes, give it to me." I said, "We asked Allah's Messenger saying, 'O Allah's Messenger! How should one (ask Allah to) send blessings on you, the members of the family, for Allah has taught us how to salute you (in the prayer)?' He said, 'Say:

اللَّهُمَّ صَلِّ عَلَى مُحَمَّدٍ وَعَلَى آلِ مُحَمَّدٍ كَمَا صَلَّيْتَ عَلَى إِبْرَاهِيمَ وَعَلَى آلِ إِبْرَاهِيمَ إِنَّكَ حَمِيدٌ مَجِيدٌ اللَّهُمَّ بَارِكْ عَلَى مُحَمَّدٍ وَعَلَى آلِ مُحَمَّدٍ كَمَا بَارَكْتَ عَلَى إِبْرَاهِيمَ وَعَلَى آلِ إِبْرَاهِيمَ إِنَّكَ حَمِيدٌ مَجِيدٌ

Allah humma ṣalli ʿalā Muḥammadin wa ʿalā āli Muḥammadin kamā ṣallayta ʿalā Ibraheema wa ʿalā āli Ibraheema innaka ḥameedum majeed. Allah humma bārik ʿalā Muḥammadin wa ʿalā āli Muḥammadin kamā bārakta ʿalā Ibraheema wa ʿalā āli Ibraheema innaka ḥameedum majeed

O Allah! Send Your Mercy on Muhammad and on the family of Muhammad, as You sent Your Mercy on Abraham and on the family of Abraham, for You are the Most Praise-worthy, the Most Glorious. O Allah! Send Your Blessings on Muhammad and the family of Muhammad, as You sent your Blessings on Abraham and on the family of Abraham, for You are the Most Praise-worthy, the Most Glorious.'"
(Sahih Bukhari)

Taqwa and Tawakkul

Allah mentions in the Qur'an the twin rays of hope for a believer: taqwa and tawakkul.

وَمَن يَتَّقِ اللَّهَ يَجْعَل لَّهُ مَخْرَجًا وَيَرْزُقْهُ مِنْ حَيْثُ لَا يَحْتَسِبُ ۚ وَمَن يَتَوَكَّلْ عَلَى اللَّهِ فَهُوَ حَسْبُهُ ۚ إِنَّ اللَّهَ بَالِغُ أَمْرِهِ ۚ قَدْ جَعَلَ اللَّهُ لِكُلِّ شَيْءٍ قَدْرًا

Whoever has taqwa of Allah – He will give him a way out and provide for him from where he does not expect. Whoever puts his trust in Allah – He will be enough for him. Allah always achieves His aim. Allah has appointed a measure for all things.

(Surah at-Talaq 65:2-3)

Taqwa means being aware of Allah, conscious of wanting to please Him and following His commands, so that you refrain from doing that which He dislikes.

اتَّقِ اللَّهِ حَيْثُمَا كُنْتَ وَأَتْبِعْ السَّيِّئَةَ الْحَسَنَةَ تَمْحُهَا وَخَالِقِ النَّاسَ بِخُلُقٍ حَسَنٍ

Abu Dharr ؓ reported that the Messenger of Allah ﷺ said:
Have taqwa of Allah wherever you are, follow a bad deed with a good deed and it will erase it, and behave with good character towards people.
(Sunan at-Tirmidhi)

Tawakkul means having full trust, dependence and reliance that His plan for you is perfect once you have put in your full efforts, as the following hadith explains:

يَا رَسُولَ اللَّهِ أَعْقِلُهَا وَأَتَوَكَّلُ أَوْ أُطْلِقُهَا وَأَتَوَكَّلُ قَالَ ﷺ اعْقِلْهَا وَتَوَكَّلْ

Anas ibn Malik ؓ reported: A man said,
"O Messenger of Allah, should I tie my camel and trust in Allah, or should I leave her untied and trust in Allah?" The Prophet, peace and blessings be upon him, said, "Tie her and trust in Allah."
(Sunan at-Tirmidhi)

It is important to note that tawakkul comes with taking steps to ensure we have done everything to ensure a good result. So if we ask for success in our exams, we must also study to the best of our abilities, make du'a and then leave the results in the Hands of Allah.

When you rely on others besides Allah ﷻ they will always fall short of your expectations and disappoint you, but if you rely on Allah ﷻ alone then you have sought help from The One Who will never let you down.

Sabr

There are numerous times in the Qur'an that the virtues of sabr have been outlined. Allah ﷻ gives glad tidings to those who have sabr and has promised that He is with them.

وَٱصْبِرُوٓا۟ إِنَّ ٱللَّهَ مَعَ ٱلصَّٰبِرِينَ

And be steadfast. Allah is with the steadfast.
(Surah al-Anfal 8:46)

Sabr means more than being patient but being consciously and actively steadfast, consistent and regular in believing, doing good deeds and staying away from that which is forbidden no matter how difficult the situation may become. This is a quality that Allah ﷻ loves (Surah Ali-Imran 3:146). So if we cultivate sabr at the time of hardship, we are essentially making ourselves beloved to Allah ﷻ.

وَاعْلَمْ أَنَّ فِي الصَّبْرِ عَلَى مَا تَكْرَهُ خَيْرًا كَثِيرًا وَأَنَّ النَّصْرَ مَعَ الصَّبْرِ وَأَنَّ الْفَرَجَ مَعَ الْكَرْبِ وَأَنَّ مَعَ الْعُسْرِ يُسْرًا

Ibn 'Abbas ؓ narrated that the Prophet ﷺ said regarding patience:
Know that there is much good in being patient with what you detest, victory will come with patience, affliction will come with relief, and "with hardship will come with ease." (94:4-5)
(Musnad Ahmed)

Patience is so central to Islam that Ibn Qayyim states:

> "Iman is in two halves: half is patience (sabr) and half is gratitude (shukr)."²²

Shukr

Gratitude is the means to gain increase.

وَإِذْ تَأَذَّنَ رَبُّكُمْ لَئِن شَكَرْتُمْ لَأَزِيدَنَّكُمْ وَلَئِن كَفَرْتُمْ إِنَّ عَذَابِى لَشَدِيدٌ

And when your Lord announced: "If you are grateful, I will certainly give you increase, but if you are ungrateful, My punishment is severe."
(Surah Ibrahim 14:7)

The same emphatic ل and نَّ which we highlighted in the beginning of this book regarding the verb 'to test' in 2:155 is used here for the verb to increase. In other words, Allah ﷻ has guaranteed that He ﷻ will certainly increase us in blessings if we are grateful to Him ﷻ.

One aspect of gratitude is to recognise that contentment does not come about when we have all that we want; it comes in appreciating what we have, being content with it and grateful for it. When we reach this state of shukr – of being thankful to Allah ﷻ at all times – then no matter what circumstances we find ourself in, the heart will be rich and the soul will be satisfied.

Ibn Taymiyyah, the thirteenth century Muslim scholar, was imprisoned and his student, Ibn Qayyim says:

---

22 Ibn Qayyim Al-Jawziyyah, trans. Nasiruddin Al-Khattab, *Patience and Gratitude* (Ta-Ha Publishers Ltd, London, 1997) p.55

I heard the Shaykh of Islam, Ibn Taymiyyah, say: Truly, there is a Heaven in this world, (and) whoever does not enter it, will not enter the Heaven of the next world. And once he said: What can my enemies do to me? I have in my breast both my Heaven and my garden. If I travel they are with me, and they never leave me. Imprisonment for me is a religious retreat (khalwa). To be slain for me is martyrdom (shahadah) and to be exiled from my land is a spiritual journey.[23]

This description of Ibn Taymiyyah's state of gratitude to Allah ﷻ even in the worst of circumstances shows the level of gratitude that Ibn Taymiyyah displayed and his appreciation of Allah's ﷻ blessings on him.

Serve the deen of Allah ﷻ

In times of difficulty and hardship, it is easy to fall into despair and self-pity and to imagine that our problems are greater than they may actually be. In order to regain perspective and balance, it is important to remember we have a purpose to fulfil in this life which has nothing to do with the accumulation of wealth, status or fame. Rather our purpose is to worship Allah ﷻ.

$$وَمَا خَلَقْتُ ٱلْجِنَّ وَٱلْإِنسَ إِلَّا لِيَعْبُدُونِ$$

I only created jinn and man to worship me.
(Surah adh-Dhariyat 51:56)

When we seek sincerely to serve the deen of Allah ﷻ then this serves the purpose of drawing closer to Allah ﷻ and earning His pleasure, as well as diverting our attention from our own problems.

---

23 Ibn Qayyim, *The Invocation of God*, p.57 cited in Aisha Utz *The Prick of a Thorn* (International Islamic Publishing House, Riyadh, 2014) p.276 also see Al-Qarni, trans. Faisal ibn Muhammad Shafeeq, *Don't be Sad* (International Islamic Publishing House, Riyadh, 2005) p.120

$$\text{يَٰٓأَيُّهَا ٱلَّذِينَ ءَامَنُوٓا۟ إِن تَنصُرُوا۟ ٱللَّهَ يَنصُرْكُمْ وَيُثَبِّتْ أَقْدَامَكُمْ}$$

> You who believe! If you help Allah, He will help you.
> (Surah Muhammad 47:7)

If Allah helps you, then none can defeat you:

$$\text{إِن يَنصُرْكُمُ ٱللَّهُ فَلَا غَالِبَ لَكُمْ ۖ وَإِن يَخْذُلْكُمْ فَمَن ذَا ٱلَّذِى يَنصُرُكُم مِّنۢ بَعْدِهِۦ ۗ وَعَلَى ٱللَّهِ فَلْيَتَوَكَّلِ ٱلْمُؤْمِنُونَ}$$

> If Allah helps you, no one can vanquish you.
> If He forsakes you, who can help you after that?
> So the believers should put their trust in Allah.
> (Surah Ali-Imran 3:160)

There are many different means by which we can serve the deen of Allah ﷻ but one means that is a particularly powerful way of alleviating one's own suffering and pain is by serving those in more challenging situations than us:

> يَا ابْنَ آدَمَ مَرِضْتُ فَلَمْ تَعُدْنِي قَالَ يَا رَبِّ كَيْفَ أَعُودُكَ وَأَنْتَ رَبُّ الْعَالَمِينَ قَالَ أَمَا عَلِمْتَ أَنَّ عَبْدِي فُلَانًا مَرِضَ فَلَمْ تَعُدْهُ أَمَا عَلِمْتَ أَنَّكَ لَوْ عُدْتَهُ لَوَجَدْتَنِي عِنْدَهُ يَا ابْنَ آدَمَ اسْتَطْعَمْتُكَ فَلَمْ تُطْعِمْنِي قَالَ يَا رَبِّ وَكَيْفَ أُطْعِمُكَ وَأَنْتَ رَبُّ الْعَالَمِينَ قَالَ أَمَا عَلِمْتَ أَنَّهُ اسْتَطْعَمَكَ عَبْدِي فُلَانٌ فَلَمْ تُطْعِمْهُ أَمَا عَلِمْتَ أَنَّكَ لَوْ أَطْعَمْتَهُ لَوَجَدْتَ ذَلِكَ عِنْدِي يَا ابْنَ آدَمَ اسْتَسْقَيْتُكَ فَلَمْ تَسْقِنِي قَالَ يَا رَبِّ كَيْفَ أَسْقِيكَ وَأَنْتَ رَبُّ الْعَالَمِينَ قَالَ اسْتَسْقَاكَ عَبْدِي فُلَانٌ فَلَمْ تَسْقِهِ أَمَا إِنَّكَ لَوْ سَقَيْتَهُ لَوَجَدْتَ ذَلِكَ عِنْدِي

Abu Huraira ﷺ narrated that the Messenger of Allah ﷺ said: *Allah ﷻ will say on the Day of Resurrection: "O son of Adam, I fell ill and you visited Me not." He will say: "O Lord, and how should I visit You when You are the Lord of the worlds?" He will say: "Did you not know that My servant So-and-so had fallen ill and you visited him not? Did you not know that had you visited him you would have found Me with him? O son of Adam, I asked you for food and you fed Me not." He will say: "O Lord, and how should I feed You when You are the Lord of the worlds?" He will say: "Did you not know that My servant So-and-so asked you for food and you fed him not? Did you not know that had you fed him you would surely have found that (the reward for doing so) with Me? O son of Adam, I asked you to give Me to drink and you gave Me not to drink." He will say: "O Lord, how should I give You to drink when You are the Lord of the worlds?" He will say: "My servant So-and-so asked you to give him to drink and you gave him not to drink. Had you given him to drink you would have surely found that with Me."* (Muslim)

Al-Qarni makes an interesting observation regarding this hadith:
... in the last third of the hadith are the words: "...you would have found Me with him"....Allah, the All-Merciful, is with those whose hearts are troubled, as is the case with the person who is sick.[24]

When we look to those less fortunate than us, we are reminded of our own abundant blessings.

انْظُرُوا إِلَى مَنْ أَسْفَلَ مِنْكُمْ وَلاَ تَنْظُرُوا إِلَى مَنْ هُوَ فَوْقَكُمْ فَهُوَ أَجْدَرُ أَنْ لاَ تَزْدَرُوا نِعْمَةَ اللَّهِ

---

[24] Al-Qarni, trans. Faisal ibn Muhammad Shafeeq, *Don't be Sad* (International Islamic Publishing House, Riyadh, 2005) p.122

Abu Huraira ﷺ narrated that the Messenger of Allah ﷺ said:
Look at those below you and do not look at those above you, for it is the best way not to belittle the favours of Allah.
(Sahih Bukhari and Muslim)

Keep company with the righteous

Our deen is not one of individualism and isolation and we are strongly encouraged to keep in the company of righteous believers.

وَٱصْبِرْ نَفْسَكَ مَعَ ٱلَّذِينَ يَدْعُونَ رَبَّهُم بِٱلْغَدَوٰةِ وَٱلْعَشِيِّ يُرِيدُونَ وَجْهَهُۥ ۖ وَلَا تَعْدُ عَيْنَاكَ عَنْهُمْ تُرِيدُ زِينَةَ ٱلْحَيَوٰةِ ٱلدُّنْيَا ۖ وَلَا تُطِعْ مَنْ أَغْفَلْنَا قَلْبَهُۥ عَن ذِكْرِنَا وَٱتَّبَعَ هَوَىٰهُ وَكَانَ أَمْرُهُۥ فُرُطًا

Restrain yourself patiently with those who call on their Lord morning and evening desiring His face. Do not turn your eyes from them, desiring the attractions of this world, And do not obey someone whose heart We have made neglectful of Our remembrance and who follows his own whims and desires and whose life has transgressed all bounds.
(Surah al-Kahf 18:28)

Keeping righteous company will steer you towards the right path whenever you begin to stray and will remind you of Allah ﷻ when you fall into a state of heedlessness. Shaytan is all too ready to whisper and convince us when we are alone and vulnerable to his suggestions.

Remember your final abode

جَنَّٰتُ عَدْنٍ يَدْخُلُونَهَا وَمَن صَلَحَ مِنْ ءَابَآئِهِمْ وَأَزْوَٰجِهِمْ وَذُرِّيَّٰتِهِمْ وَٱلْمَلَٰٓئِكَةُ يَدْخُلُونَ عَلَيْهِم مِّن كُلِّ بَابٍ

سَلَٰمٌ عَلَيْكُم بِمَا صَبَرْتُمْ فَنِعْمَ عُقْبَى ٱلدَّارِ

Gardens of Eden which they will enter, and all of their parents, wives and children who were righteous. Angels will enter in to welcome then from every gate: "Peace be upon you because of your steadfastness! How wonderful is the ultimate abode!"

(Surah ar-Rad 13:23-24)

Know that whatever you are going through in this life will soon end and the abode of the afterlife is waiting. A place of eternity. For the righteous, a place where there is no suffering, no hatred, no sickness, no anger, no pain. A place of unfathomable beauty, greater than any pleasure that can be conceived by the human mind. A place where the righteous will be blessed with the greatest blessing of all; they will be granted the vision of The Most Compassionate, The Most Merciful, The Lord of all that exists, Allah ﷻ.

هَلْ جَزَآءُ ٱلْإِحْسَٰنِ إِلَّا ٱلْإِحْسَٰنُ

Will the reward for doing good be anything other than good?
(Surah ar-Rahman 55:60)

Recommended Reading

- Al-'Ubudiyyah: Being a True Slave of Allah *by Ibn Taymiyah*
- Patience and Gratitude *by Ibn Taymiyah*
- The Intelligent Heart, The Pure Heart *by Gohar Mushtaq*
- Slaves of the All-Merciful *by Mohsen Shaker Al-Bayoumi*
- A Concise Description of Jannah and Jahannam *by Shaikh Abd Al-Qadir Al-Jilani*
- The Life of Muhammad ﷺ *by Tahia al-Ismail*

All available from **www.tahapublishers.com**